TRANSITIONAL RURAL LANDSCAPES

Socio-Environmental Dynamics, Economic Performances and Climate Change

EDITED BY

IOANNIS KONAXIS

University of Piraeus, Greece

AND

LUCA SALVATI

Sapienza University of Rome, Italy

emerald
PUBLISHING

United Kingdom – North America – Japan – India
Malaysia – China

Emerald Publishing Limited
Emerald Publishing, Floor 5, Northspring, 21-23 Wellington Street, Leeds LS1 4DL.

First edition 2026

British Library Cataloguing in Publication Data
A catalogue record for this book is available from the British Library

ISBN: 978-1-80592-894-2 (Print)
ISBN: 978-1-80592-893-5 (Online)
ISBN: 978-1-80592-895-9 (Epub)

Printed and bound by CPI Group (UK) Ltd, Croydon, CR0 4YY

INVESTOR IN PEOPLE

CONTENTS

ABOUT THE EDITORS

Ioannis Konaxis, PhD in Landscape Architecture, is Assistant Professor at the Department of Tourism Studies, University of Piraeus, Greece. He is an expert in landscape analysis, urban dynamics, tourism expansion and local development. He has published several scientific articles and professional reports for Greece and the European Union.

Luca Salvati, PhD in Economics, is Associate Professor of Applied Economics and Economic Statistics (Full Staff) at the Department of Methods and Models for Economics, Territory and Finance, Faculty of Economics, Sapienza University of Rome, Italy. He has published more than 800 international publications, including several books realised with international publishers.

ABOUT THE CONTRIBUTORS

Ahmed Alhussen is Senior Research Fellow at the Global Change Research Institute of the Czech Academy of Sciences, Czech Republic.

Leonardo Bianchini is Tenure-track Researcher at the Department of Agricultural and Forestry Sciences, Tuscia University, Viterbo, Italy.

Clio Ciaschini is Senior Research Fellow at the Department of Economics and Social Science, Polytechnic University of Marche, Ancona, Italy.

Giuseppe Cillis is Senior Research Fellow at National Research Council of Italy (CNR), Institute of Methodologies for Environmental Analysis (IMAA), Tito Scalo, Italy.

Rosa Coluzzi is Senior Researcher at National Research Council of Italy (CNR), Institute of Methodologies for Environmental Analysis (IMAA), Tito Scalo, Italy.

Jesus Rodrigo Comino is Associate Professor of Geography at the Departamento de Análisis Geográfico Regional y Geografía Física, Facultad de Filosofía y Letras, Campus Universitario de Cartuja, Universidad de Granada, Spain.

Yuri Corradi is Staff Statistician at Italian National Statistical Institute, Rome, Italy.

Alessia D'Agata is PhD candidate at the Department of Methods and Models for Economics, Territory and Finance (MEMOTEF), Faculty of Economics, Sapienza University of Rome, Italy.

Mariagrazia D'Emilio is Senior Researcher at Italian National Research Council of Italy (CNR), Institute of Methodologies for Environmental Analysis (IMAA), Tito Scalo, Italy.

Gianluca Egidi is Research Fellow at the Department of Agricultural and Forestry Sciences (DAFNE), University of Tuscia, Viterbo, Italy.

Luigi Fici is Full Professor of Business Economics at the Department of Economics, Engineering, Society and Business Organization, Tuscia University, Viterbo, Italy.

Vito Imbrenda is Senior Researcher at National Research Council of Italy (CNR), Institute of Methodologies for Environmental Analysis (IMAA), Tito Scalo, Italy.

Maria Lanfredi is Senior Researcher at National Research Council of Italy (CNR), Institute of Methodologies for Environmental Analysis (IMAA), Tito Scalo, Italy.

Marco Maialetti is an Independent Researcher and Lawyer based in Rome, Italy.

Maurizio Masi is Associate Professor of Business Economics at the Department of Economics, Engineering, Society and Business Organization, Tuscia University, Viterbo, Italy.

Nadia Matarazzo is Associate Professor of Geography at the Department of Economic and Statistical Sciences, 'Federico II' University, Naples, Italy.

Bogdana Nosova is Adjunct Professor at the Department of Social Communications, and previous Assistant Professor at the Department of International Journalism and the Department of Social Communications, Institute of Journalism, Taras Shevchenko National University of Kyiv, Ukraine.

Letizia Pace is Research Fellow at the Department of Earth and Geoenvironmental Sciences, University of Bari Aldo Moro, Italy.

Giovanni Quaranta is Full Professor of Agricultural Economics at the Department of Mathematics, Computer Science and Economics, University of Basilicata, Italy.

Rosanna Salvia is Associate Professor of Agricultural economics at the Department of Mathematics, Computer Science and Economics, University of Basilicata, Italy.

Caterina Samela is Researcher at National Research Council of Italy (CNR), Institute of Methodologies for Environmental Analysis (IMAA), Tito Scalo, Italy.

Adele Sateriano is an Independent Researcher affiliated with Mediterranean Sustainable Development Foundation (MEDES), Salerno, Italy.

Donato Scarpitta is an Independent Researcher and Architect based in Salerno, Italy.

Tiziana Simoniello is Senior Researcher at National Research Council of Italy (CNR), Institute of Methodologies for Environmental Analysis (IMAA), Tito Scalo, Italy.

1

TOWARD AGRO-ECOLOGICAL SUSTAINABILITY? ANALYZING COMPLEX SOCIO-ENVIRONMENTAL DYNAMICS IN RURAL LANDSCAPES

ROSANNA SALVIA[a], GIOVANNI QUARANTA[a], AHMED ALHUSSEN[b], MARCO MAIALETTI[c], DONATO SCARPITTA[d], ADELE SATERIANO[e], IOANNIS KONAXIS[f] AND LUCA SALVATI[g]

[a]University of Basilicata, Italy
[b]Global Change Research Institute of the Czech Academy of Sciences, Czech Republic
[c]Independent Researcher and Lawyer, Italy
[d]Independent Researcher and Architect, Italy
[e]Independent Researcher Affiliated with Mediterranean Sustainable Development Foundation (MEDES), Italy
[f]University of Piraeus, Greece
[g]Sapienza University of Rome, Italy

ABSTRACT

Agricultural landscapes have evolved in the last century at a much faster rate than in the recent past. The present work discusses all these processes, evaluating agricultural decline not only in economically marginal, mountainous, or scarcely accessible areas, but also considering more accessible areas, economically suited to trade and industrial production. They have been hit by specific phenomena of "speculative expectation" which, in many cases, have led to low-density urbanization with a mix of land uses leading to an entropic and indefinite form of peri-urban landscapes. In anthropogenic landscapes, where land consumption emerges as the sole outcome of "one-way" socioeconomic development paths, it is crucial that environmental policies combine strict regulatory measures with sustained efforts to create land suitable for specific activities such as tourism, services, crafts, and high-quality agri-food production. These measures should necessarily be accompanied by incentives, professional training, and (local) development support, aimed both at revitalizing economically and socially depressed areas, thereby reducing their exposure to fragmented urbanization.

Keywords: Socio-ecological systems; ecological sustainability; Mediterranean basin; statistical indicators; landscape change

INTRODUCTION

The incorporation of cognitive and complexity-oriented perspectives into the analysis of socioeconomic networks has profoundly reshaped the prevailing interpretations of complex territorial dynamics. These perspectives move beyond static or reductionist representations by emphasizing the endogenous emergence of spatial and organizational structures driven by adaptive, learning agents. Central to this line of inquiry is the recognition that localized interactions, operating through distributed decision-making processes, can give rise to persistent centers of attraction, novel spatial configurations, and cumulative processes of innovation (Batty & Longley, 1994). Such insights have become increasingly salient in contemporary regional contexts marked by growing discontinuities between urban and rural areas, sustained economic instability, and significant transformations in social values, institutional arrangements, and political–regulatory frameworks.

Within this evolving context, regional systems are increasingly conceptualized as open, adaptive, and non-linear entities, whose development trajectories cannot be adequately captured by equilibrium-based or centrally coordinated models. Rather, their evolution unfolds through complex feedback mechanisms involving anticipatory agents who continuously adjust their strategies in response to endogenous interactions and exogenous signals, thereby contributing to the ongoing reconfiguration of spatial units and functional relations (Holland, 2006). Importantly, the complexity observed at the regional scale does not arise from the sophistication of individual actors, but from the aggregation and interaction of relatively simple behavioral rules operating across space and time.

These decentralized interactions generate emergent spatial outcomes that may be examined along two analytically distinct yet mutually reinforcing dimensions. The first is a morphological dimension, encompassing transformations in spatial form, settlement patterns, and territorial configurations (Oliveira, 2016). The second is a functional dimension, reflecting the evolving spatial distribution of economic activities, institutional functions, and social practices (Burger & Meijers, 2012). Both dimensions are shaped by iterative processes of individual and collective choice, reciprocal feedback among social actors, and the adaptive strategies of economic agents engaged in competitive, cooperative, and co-evolutionary relationships. As a result, the spatial organization of economic activity should be understood as a dynamic and historically contingent process, reflecting relational structures between places rather than stable or optimal spatial equilibria (Berry, 2005).

From an analytical and empirical standpoint, the intrinsically relational and multilevel nature of regional systems presents substantial challenges for their evaluation and measurement. The interdependence of processes operating at different spatial and organizational scales complicates attempts to isolate causal mechanisms or to assess system performance through conventional indicators (Cumming et al., 2006). Nevertheless, comparative evidence from both urban and rural contexts suggests that, despite substantial heterogeneity, regional systems often exhibit convergent evolutionary patterns over time. These patterns include processes of variation, selection, imitation, learning, and adaptive reorientation in response to changing environmental, economic, and institutional conditions (Kourtit et al., 2014).

Such regularities point to development dynamics that are predominantly self-organizing, emerging from localized interactions rather than from hierarchical control or centralized planning. Even when exposed to significant external pressures – such as climate change, demographic transitions, or macroeconomic shocks – regional systems frequently demonstrate an inherent capacity for structural adjustment and functional reorganization (Simmie & Martin, 2010). This capacity underpins their long-term resilience and sustainability, which are not imposed exogenously but instead arise endogenously from the configuration of local networks, institutional diversity, and adaptive behavioral responses (Turgel & Chernova, 2024).

On the basis of these theoretical premises, the present contribution adopts a multidisciplinary analytical perspective to examine selected complex processes and localized territorial systems. By integrating environmental considerations with empirically grounded and economically relevant case studies, the analysis seeks to bridge complexity theory and operational concerns in spatial planning and regional development. The overarching objective is to demonstrate that complex systems thinking constitutes not only a robust framework for scientific analysis but also a critical foundation for the formulation of policy approaches capable of addressing uncertainty, fostering adaptability, and enhancing the resilience of regional systems.

The Inherent Evolution in Advanced Economic Systems

Starting from World War II, developed countries experienced deep transformations in land use, along with economic development. These changes affected both natural and anthropogenic environments, progressively altering the traits of extensiveness and environmental sustainability that had defined rural systems until the 1950s. Throughout the last century, agricultural landscapes have undergone changes far more rapidly compared with the previous time periods (Winkler et al., 2021). At present, this evolution process has accelerated even further (Fig. 1.1).

Among other drivers, the sudden urbanization of sea coasts and the continuous industrialization of inland areas, the construction of infrastructures

Fig. 1.1. A Representative Illustration of Mixed and Fragmented Rural Landscapes Under Increasing Anthropogenic Pressure in the Mediterranean Region.

Source: Authors' Photographic Archive.

and the consequent sprawl of low-density settlements, have significantly influenced the evolution of rural areas toward urbanization, industrialization, and "touristification" (Cillis et al., 2025; Gedecho et al., 2025; Siddik & Islam, 2024). This may also result in a persistent shift of the economy toward more advanced tertiary sectors, implying relevant transformations in consumer lifestyles, both in urban and agricultural areas (Imbrenda, Gómez, et al., 2023). Moreover, starting from the 1970s, the role of agriculture as a "functional defence," basically for accessible areas closer to the city, has been significantly challenged. Due to mechanization, fertilization, irrigation, and systems with a greater impact on land, crop intensification leads to "single-crop" landscapes, observed still today, sometimes in connection with the inherent scarcity of natural elements (Meehan et al., 2011).

Based on this disciplinary positioning, the present work specifically evaluates such phenomena considering the functional and structural decline of agriculture as a process not only limited to economically marginal, mountainous, or less accessible areas, but also involving more accessible territories specialized in trade and industry. These areas experienced well-known dynamics of "speculative expectation," in many cases favoring low-density urbanization forms and heterogeneous land uses shaping peri-urban (fragmented) landscapes without a defined configuration.

Faced with such pervasive changes, even if diluted over a consistent time interval, diachronic statistical information – fueling the creation and dissemination of useful indicators that can inform urban, socioeconomic, agricultural, and environmental policies – perhaps it still appears lacking (Huang et al., 2024). This appears in several European contexts, especially in the Mediterranean countries, and results from sometimes ambiguous definitions, and an ups and downs interest (or awareness) in arguments dealing with ecology, landscape, and territory (Carletto, 2021).

Within this framework, variables associated with areas destined to agricultural, urban, and industrial purposes, widened roads and railways, and the pressure from human settlements along with urban sprawl, the loss of agricultural and forest land, intensified farming practices, or the depopulation of rural areas, are revealed as crucial determinants of local development and landscape transformations. Over a long-term perspective, these factors become crucial in every decision dealing with territorial management, safeguard of traditional landscapes, containment of soil consumption, and economic valorization of arable land.

Pervasive Changes, Intrinsic Problems

A deeper multi-disciplinary knowledge on soil quality would be achieved integrating classical evaluations of agronomic and economic nature with quantitative (physical) estimations and monetary assessment of ecosystem services (Carlucci et al., 2022). These estimates allow for the evaluation of the environmental conditions to design territorial policies favoring urban containment, e.g., allowing new settlements in areas less (economically, agronomically, and environmentally) impacting, thus stimulating urban recovery in other contexts with "judiciously compact" settlements (Fig. 1.2). The lack of diachronic evaluations, connected with the spatial limitation and the restricted temporal comparability of some statistical sources (including those provided by general censuses of population, buildings, industry, or agriculture), brings to the few indicators covering the time period from the aftermath of World War II to present times (Li et al., 2023).

By highlighting an evident deterioration of environmental conditions, this trend goes along with the productive transformations that have shaped these dynamics, particularly in agricultural regions with greater accessibility. In both cases, urbanization – recently characterized by dispersed and fragmented patterns – has been the main driver (directly or indirectly) causing the upheavals mentioned above. A slow but continuous change in socio-demographic and economic conditions has been associated with the territorial context and its morphological transformations, including population decline, especially in rural areas, the abandonment of less productive land, and increasing settlement concentration (Hospers & Reverda, 2015; Li & Li, 2017; Ragosta et al., 2024).

Fig. 1.2. Urbanization Signs in Mediterranean Rural Landscapes.

Source: Authors' Photographic Archive.

Since the last 50 years, landscape evolution has also been affected by European-driven (or, at least, inspired) agricultural policies (Lefebvre et al., 2012). In particular, the production support, characterizing the European Union (EU) governmental policies, along with progressive urbanization and industrialization, impacted agricultural land use within several production contexts (Ustaoglu & Williams, 2022). Moreover, the recent EU agricultural policies resulted in two forms of agriculture, i.e., (i) an economically strong and market-oriented "productive" model, and (ii) a form inspired by environmental protection, oriented toward the optimal management of rural space, local realities, and the promotion of traditional agricultural activities.

At the same time, environmental policies, designed and applied at various operational scales, from local to national, have represented opportunities, sometimes isolated, sometimes connected with spatial planning, stimulating forms of sustainable local development in rural areas that became progressively more urbanized (Coluzzi et al., 2022). In (highly or moderately) anthropogenic contexts, where land consumption emerges as the sole outcome of a "one-way" socioeconomic development, environmental policies should design strict regulatory measures aimed at creating areas suitable for crafts, tourism activities, and research purposes, as well as producing high-quality agri-food industries (Imbrenda, Coluzzi, et al., 2023).

These provisions should be promoted through professional training and economic incentives to revitalize depressed areas, preserving them from fragmented urbanization (Cicco et al., 2025). The success of these policies relies on the subsistence of an effective, sustainable socioeconomic development strategy (Fig. 1.3), characterized by multiple factors capturing the intrinsic evolution of the interaction between each local community and its available natural resources. This also requires coordinated and effective sectoral policies (Lanfredi et al., 2023).

A "MANIFESTO" FOR RURAL LANDSCAPES

Territorial resources should be managed in a sustainable way, considering the natural landscape and the preservation of biodiversity as joint issues. In this perspective, Chapter 2 delineates the crucial challenge of our millennium, namely the contextual development of human beings and Earth's ecosystem. Moreover, Chapter 3 analyzes the long-term impact of climate and soil aridity on ecologically fragile agricultural systems, jointly investigating rainfall and temperature regimes – considering the empirical results of quantitative analysis of meteorological time series at both national and regional scales.

Fig. 1.3. Soil Crusting, Southern Sicily.

Source: Authors' Photographic Archive.

Accordingly, it suggests new paradigms to prevent climate aridity and droughts in rural and natural environments at different observation scales adopting innovative tools and indicators (e.g., Ferretti et al., 2014).

Environmental Challenges

The "environmental syndrome" defines a set of interactive processes and symptoms repeatedly occurring in peculiar combinations and patterns. Land degradation (LD) results in a persistent reduction or loss in the capacity of land to provide ecosystem services (Imbrenda et al., 2013). Its occurrence can be described with specific Land-Use/Land Cover Changes, seen as (sustainable or unsustainable) trajectories of landscape transformations (Fig. 1.4).

Within this framework, Chapter 4 delves into the "syndrome" concept to highlight its complexity in LD processes, through scenario analysis based on past environmental conditions. The main results of this analysis should be the starting point to develop Sustainable Land Management strategies. Evaluating the health conditions of ecosystem services of a given area supports the assessment of LD effects. By establishing associations with significant LD syndromes, this work focused on the identification of past land-use trajectories (Pace et al., 2023).

Socioeconomic Challenges

An exhaustive evaluation of economic and socio-demographic dynamics over longer time periods could not rescind from a careful analysis of the related

Fig. 1.4. Dry Natural Landscapes in the Northern Mediterranean Region.
Source: Authors' Photographic Archive.

environmental context. Chapter 5 examines the intricate relationship between forests, shrublands, and other forms of land use, such as agricultural areas and pastures as well as urban and industrial zones. The high level of complexity of these interactions directly affects the ecosystems' ability to provide, at the same time, a wide range of diversified ecosystem services. Proper and effective management methods are, therefore, required to address the issue, particularly given their high social, economic, and ecological importance, illustrated through a practical case in Southern Italy. Finally, Chapter 6 investigates the behavior of Italian households regarding separate waste collection and their perception of some specific aspects of this complex environmental problem, such as the accessibility of differentiated waste collection bins, with a specific focus on rural areas. This issue – addressing societal needs – may complete the interpretative path from economics to society, addressing the environmental problems underlying the central chapters of this book (Fig. 1.5).

THE RELEVANCE OF "TERRITORIALIZATION" PROCESSES

Within rural contexts, environmental syndromes seem to represent "the pathology of the relationship between social organizations and the biophysical characteristics of natural ecosystems". To some extent, degradation and

Fig. 1.5. An Illegal Waste Dump Close to Informal Settlements.

Source: Authors' Photographic Archive.

its determinants seem to adhere to the forms of feedback (adaptation processes) identified in systems theory. At the very local level, LD relates to the territorial action of human societies, so it is impossible to imagine forms of "territorialization" without negative externalities, looking at the characteristics of the natural ecosystems (Imbrenda et al., 2024). Nevertheless, the system's feedback to the territorial evolutionary trends and the process of degradation calls for a careful interpretation of the effects of soil degradation processes both under ecological and socioeconomic perspectives.

Going from regional to local, the chapters briefly introduced before may provide examples of a multi-scale analysis of environmental change giving appropriate opportunities to ascertain the combined effect of socio-demographic dynamics on urbanization, evidencing the role of social transformations and the latent linkage with "hegemonic" concepts such as that of LD, which is intimately related with both socioeconomic dynamics and environmental sustainability. Reconnecting impacts of regional-scale socioeconomic change with local-scale ecological dynamics definitely contributes to an enriched knowledge of environmental histories, outlining how a study of differences under assumptions of non-linearity and complex system thinking is key to understanding future socio-environmental trends (Fig. 1.6).

Therefore, a strong significance resides in the extent to which degradation processes, arising from specific forms of "territorialization," affect the socioeconomic organization of entire regions. Analytically, a multidisciplinary investigation methodology should identify those functional or structural links characterizing the processes of "territorialization" of the geographical space

Fig. 1.6. Natural and Human-Derived Degradation of Dunes and Retro-Dune Habitats Along the Dry Tyrrhenian Sea Coast in Central Italy.

Source: Authors' Photographic Archive.

and the related degradation processes, acquiring significant interpretative relevance for historiographical, sociological, and political-economic data. Therefore, the present work not only describes and measures landscape transformations, but also delineates the territorial historical path, focusing on the main dynamics that affect landscape features in advanced economies, and more specifically in the Northern Mediterranean basin.

In line with this theoretical assumption, contemporary research investigates both overt and latent relationships in the transformation of landscapes and land-use systems across advanced economies, emphasizing the interactions between demographic shifts, economic restructuring, and climate change. By adopting a comparative and multi-scalar perspective, such inquiry addresses the complex dynamics shaping urban, agricultural, and forested areas under increasing uncertainty regarding exogenous drivers, whether environmental, economic, or socio-political. This work is inherently trans-disciplinary, situated at the interface of environmental, social, and economic sciences, and emphasizes the integration of multiple analytical perspectives to understand and manage complex territorial systems.

This line of inquiry is particularly relevant to sustainable regional development, social cohesion, climate adaptation, biodiversity conservation, and energy transition. By combining methodological approaches from environmental sciences with socioeconomic analysis, it produces knowledge that is operationally relevant for regional and local planning (Pricope et al., 2023). Such research contributes to the development of strategies capable of reconciling ecological, economic, and social objectives, supporting decision-making in multi-level governance contexts across advanced economies (Fig. 1.7).

A central aim of this research is to systematize knowledge from diverse disciplines to advance sustainable development, economic vitality, and social well-being in rural and semi-natural landscapes experiencing demographic decline and socioeconomic transformation. These transformations, while presenting challenges, also offer opportunities to reinforce the role of rural landscapes as engines of regional development, providing essential ecological services, economic resources, and social benefits to surrounding communities. Forests and other natural resources, for instance, are key to supporting local livelihoods, recreation and tourism, and the sustainable production of regionally distinctive goods, while simultaneously contributing to climate mitigation and ecosystem resilience.

Fig. 1.7. Traditional Rural Landscapes Mixing Cropland and Relict Woodlots and Assuring Balanced Ecosystem Functions.

Source: Authors' Photographic Archive.

Analytical approaches integrate statistical analysis of demographic and economic indicators, remote sensing and land-use mapping, and comprehensive literature synthesis to examine long-term spatial and temporal relationships between socioeconomic change and landscape dynamics. Particular attention is given to forest expansion and management practices, including the ecological consequences of land abandonment, population aging, and increasing vulnerability to hazards such as wildfires. These analyses support the identification of priority areas where landscape change is most pronounced and where interventions may be required to sustain ecosystem services and local economic and social well-being.

Building on these insights, research in this field seeks to develop integrated strategies for the sustainable management of forested, agricultural, and peri-urban landscapes in response to demographic transitions and socioeconomic transformations (Fig. 1.8). Such strategies emphasize ecological sustainability, reduction of land abandonment risks, preservation of environmental quality, enhancement of community well-being, and the promotion of economic opportunities through sustainable tourism and the valorization of local products. By linking scientific knowledge to actionable planning frameworks, this approach produces outputs that inform regional and local policy, land-use governance, and landscape planning.

Fig. 1.8. Mixed Mediterranean Agro-Forest Landscapes Exposed to Moderate Anthropogenic Pressure.

Source: Authors' Photographic Archive.

Ultimately, this body of research contributes to a holistic understanding of rural and natural landscapes in advanced economies, providing a framework to address contemporary challenges such as demographic shifts, urbanization pressures, and climate change. By integrating multi-disciplinary perspectives and offering a comprehensive interpretation of land-use and landscape dynamics, it advances both scientific understanding and practical guidance for the sustainable governance of complex territorial systems.

CONCLUDING REMARKS

Although urbanization has traditionally dominated analyses of economic development and demographic change, increasing attention is being directed toward rural areas and natural landscapes, which play a pivotal role in shaping sustainable regional trajectories (Roldan et al., 2023). Rural territories are not merely residual spaces influenced by urban centers; they are dynamic environments undergoing profound transformations driven by demographic restructuring, evolving livelihood strategies, and the complex interplay between human activity and ecological systems (Matarazzo et al., 2025). These transformations unfold heterogeneously across regions, reflecting disparities in population distribution, economic activity, institutional capacity, and environmental vulnerability (OECD, 2025). The resulting implications for landscape integrity, resource management, and long-term sustainability are significant and increasingly intersect with regional planning challenges.

In regions with rich socio-environmental histories, such as the Mediterranean basin, conventional metrics of population growth or urban expansion often conceal the differentiated trajectories of rural spaces. Some areas experience depopulation, land abandonment, or reforestation, whereas others face agricultural intensification, environmental pressures, or rapid economic restructuring. These divergent patterns are shaped not only by biophysical constraints but also by social structures, market dynamics, historical land-use practices, and governance regimes (Gallardo et al., 2023). Understanding such heterogeneity requires analytical frameworks that integrate structural drivers with localized, context-specific processes, environmental conditions, and the broader objectives of regional planning (Maialetti et al., 2024).

A critical dimension of contemporary rural transformation is the growing influence of climate change. Shifts in temperature and precipitation patterns, increasing frequency of extreme weather events, and heightened pressure on water and soil resources interact with existing socioeconomic and ecological processes, exacerbating vulnerability and shaping the adaptive capacity of rural communities. Climate change acts as both a multiplier of existing disparities and a catalyst for new patterns of land-use change, affecting agricultural productivity, ecosystem services, and the resilience of natural landscapes (IPCC, 2023). Consequently, regional planning and rural development strategies must explicitly account for climate-related risks to ensure sustainable territorial management and long-term landscape resilience (Kauffman & Hill, 2021).

To address these complexities, research and planning efforts must adopt multi-scalar, interdisciplinary approaches that link socio-demographic and economic processes with environmental dynamics and climate variability. Analyses spanning regional to local scales enable the identification of cumulative, path-dependent, and nonlinear effects of demographic shifts, economic restructuring, and climatic pressures on land management, landscape patterns, and ecosystem functioning. Incorporating complex systems thinking allows planners and researchers to recognize feedback mechanisms in which socioeconomic change alters environmental conditions, which in turn shape future human decision-making and spatial development (Perrin et al. 2018; Bajocco et al. 2016; Bajocco et al. 2015; Biasi et al. 2015).

Integrating regional socioeconomic transformations with local ecological and landscape dynamics also enhances the understanding of rural environmental histories and resilience pathways. Historical legacies, governance frameworks, and adaptive land-use strategies interact with climate pressures to influence contemporary landscape configurations and determine the capacity of rural regions to respond to emerging challenges (Cecchini et al. 2019; Chianucci et al. 2020;Chirici et al. 2020; Ciommi et al. 2018; Corona et al. 2016). Regional planning, in this context, emerges as a crucial tool for mediating these interactions, guiding land-use allocation, supporting ecosystem-based management, and coordinating interventions that enhance both ecological sustainability and community resilience (Kim et al., 2017).

On this basis, there is a clear need to advance a multidisciplinary research and planning agenda focused on rural development, natural landscapes, and climate-adaptive strategies (Delfanti et al. 2016; Duvernoy et al. 2018; Fares et al. 2017; Kosmas et al. 2016; Nocentini et al.2017; Recanatesi et al. 2015). By combining theoretical innovation with empirical investigation, comparative case studies, and systematic literature reviews, such an approach can generate robust analytical frameworks capable of informing both science and policy (Rondeux et al. 2012; Salvati & Zitti 2007; Salvati & Zitti 2009; Salvati et al. 2012). Ultimately, this perspective supports the design of regional planning strategies and rural development policies that enhance landscape resilience, foster sustainable land-use practices, mitigate climate risks, and reinforce the long-term social, economic, and ecological viability of rural territories (Salvati et al. 2008; Zambon et al.2018; Zambon et al. 2017).

REFERENCES

Bajocco, S., Ceccarelli, T., Smiraglia, D., Salvati, L., & Ricotta, C. (2016). Modeling the ecological niche of long-term land use changes: The role of biophysical factors. *Ecological Indicators*, *60*, 231–236. https://doi.org/10.1016/j.ecolind.2015.06.034

Bajocco, S., Dragoz, E., Gitas, I., Smiraglia, D., Salvati, L., & Ricotta, C. (2015). Mapping forest fuels through vegetation phenology: The role of coarse-resolution satellite time-series. *PLOS ONE*, *10*(3), e0119811. https://doi.org/10.1371/journal.pone.0119811

Batty, M., & Longley, P. (1994). *Fractal cities*. Academic Press.

Berry, B. J. L. (2005). Cities as systems within systems of cities. *Papers in Regional Science*, *13*, 147–163.

Biasi, R., Brunori, E., Smiraglia, D., & Salvati, L. (2015). Linking traditional tree-crop landscapes and agro-biodiversity in central Italy using a database of typical and traditional products: A multiple risk assessment through a data mining analysis. *Biodiversity and Conservation*, *24*(12), 3009–3031. https://doi.org/10.1007/s10531-015-0994-5

Burger, M., & Meijers, E. (2012). Form follows function? Linking morphological and functional polycentricity. *Urban Studies*, *49*(5), 1127–1149.

Carletto, C. (2021). Better data, higher impact: Improving agricultural data systems for societal change. *European Review of Agricultural Economics*, *48*(4), 719–740.

Carlucci, M., Salvia, R., Quaranta, G., Salvati, L., & Imbrenda, V. (2022). Official statistics, spatio-temporal dynamics and local-scale monitoring: Toward integrated environmental-economic accounting for land degradation. *Letters in Spatial and Resource Sciences*, *15*(3), 469–491. https://doi.org/10.1007/s12076-022-00319-y.

Cecchini, M., Zambon, I., Pontrandolfi, A., Turco, R., Colantoni, A., Mavrakis, A., & Salvati, L. (2019). Urban sprawl and the 'olive' landscape: Sustainable land management for 'crisis' cities. *GeoJournal*, *84*(1), 237–255. https://doi.org/10.1007/s10708-018-9848-5

Chianucci, F., Puletti, N., Grotti, M., Bisaglia, C., Giannetti, F., Romano, E., Brambilla, M., Mattioli, W., Cabassi, G., Bajocco, S., Li, L., Chirici, G., Corona, P., & Tattoni, C. (2020). Influence of image pixel resolution on canopy cover estimation in poplar plantations from field, aerial and satellite optical imagery. *Annals of Silvicultural Research*, *46*(1). https://doi.org/10.12899/asr-2074

Chirici, G., Giannetti, F., McRoberts, R. E., Travaglini, D., Pecchi, M., Maselli, F., Chiesi, M., & Corona, P. (2020). Wall-to-wall spatial prediction of growing stock volume based on Italian National Forest Inventory plots and remotely sensed data. *International Journal of Applied Earth Observation and Geoinformation*, *84*, 101959. https://doi.org/10.1016/j.jag.2019.101959

Cicco, N., Candido, V., Coluzzi, R., Imbrenda, V., Lanfredi, M., Larocca, M., Lorusso, A., Benelli, C., & Sofo, A. (2025). Revitalizing marginal areas of Basilicata (Southern Italy) with saffron: A strategy approach mixing alternative cultivation system and land suitability analysis. *Land*, *14*(4), 902. https://doi.org/10.3390/land14040902

Cillis, G., Coluzzi, R., Salvati, L., Colantoni, A., Nosava, B., Imbrenda, V., & Lanfredi, M. (2025). Water resource management in tourism hotspot: A cost-effective, semi-automatic method for monitoring the diffusion of residential swimming pools. *Ecological Informatics*, 103333.

Ciommi, M., Chelli, F. M., Carlucci, M., & Salvati, L. (2018). Urban growth and demographic dynamics in Southern Europe: Toward a new statistical approach to regional science. *Sustainability*, *10*(8), 2765. https://doi.org/10.3390/su10082765

Coluzzi, R., Bianchini, L., Egidi, G., Cudlin, P., Imbrenda, V., Salvati, L., & Lanfredi, M. (2022). Density matters? Settlement expansion and land degradation in Peri-urban and rural districts of Italy. *Environmental Impact Assessment Review*, *92*, 106703. https://doi.org/10.1016/j.eiar.2021.106703

Corona, P., Cutini, A., Chiavetta, U., & Paoletti, E. (2016). Forest-food nexus: A topical opportunity for human well-being and silviculture. *Annals of Silvicultural Research*, *40*(1). https://doi.org/10.12899/asr-1181

Cumming, G. S., Cumming, D. H., & Redman, C. L. (2006). Scale mismatches in social-ecological systems: causes, consequences, and solutions. *Ecology and Society*, *11*(1), 1–10.

Delfanti, L., Colantoni, A., Recanatesi, F., Bencardino, M., Sateriano, A., Zambon, I., & Salvati, L. (2016). Solar plants, environmental degradation and local socioeconomic contexts: A case study in a Mediterranean country. *Environmental Impact Assessment Review*, *61*, 88–93. https://doi.org/10.1016/j.eiar.2016.07.003

Duvernoy, I., Zambon, I., Sateriano, A., & Salvati, L. (2018). Pictures from the other side of the fringe: Urban growth and peri-urban agriculture in a post-industrial city (Toulouse, France). *Journal of Rural Studies*, *57*, 25–35. https://doi.org/10.1016/j.jrurstud.2017.10.007

Fares, S., Bajocco, S., Salvati, L., Camarretta, N., Dupuy, J.-L., Xanthopoulos, G., Guijarro, M., Madrigal, J., Hernando, C., & Corona, P. (2017). Characterizing potential wildland fire fuel in live vegetation in the Mediterranean region. *Annals of Forest Science*, *74*(1). https://doi.org/10.1007/s13595-016-0599-5

Ferretti, M., Marchetto, A., Arisci, S., Bussotti, F., Calderisi, M., Carnicelli, S., Cecchini, G., Fabbio, G., Bertini, G., Matteucci, G., de Cinti, B., Salvati, L., & Pompei, E. (2014). On the tracks of Nitrogen deposition effects on temperate forests at their southern European range–an observational study from Italy. *Global Change Biology*, *20*(11), 3423–3438.

Gallardo, M., Fernández-Portela, J., Cocero, D., & Vilar, L. (2023). Land use and land cover changes in depopulated areas of Mediterranean Europe: A case study in two inland provinces of Spain. *Land*, *12*(11), 1967.

Gedecho, K. A., Yasin, A. S., Kovács, B. H., & Bacsi, Z. (2025). Rural tourism and land use: Unveiling global research trends, gaps, and future pathways. *Land*, *14*(10), 1934.

Holland, J. H. (2006). Studying complex adaptive systems. *Journal of Systems Science and Complexity*, *19*(1), 1–8.

Hospers, G. J., & Reverda, N. (2015). *Managing population decline in Europe's urban and rural areas* (pp. 10–14). Springer International Publishing.

Huang, G., Chen, L., Grove, M., Zhou, W., & Pickett, S. (2024). Lack of social data hinders integrative urban ecology research: Obstacles and opportunities. *Landscape Ecology*, *39*(4), 89.

Imbrenda, V., Coluzzi, R., Mariani, F., Nosova, B., Cudlinova, E., Salvia, R., Quaranta, G., Salvati, L., & Lanfredi, M. (2023). Working in (slow) progress: Socio-environmental and economic dynamics in the forestry sector and the contribution to sustainable development in Europe. *Sustainability*, *15*(13), 10271. https://doi.org/10.3390/su151310271

Imbrenda, V., D'Emilio, M., Lanfredi, M., Ragosta, M., & Simoniello, T. (2013). Indicators of land degradation vulnerability due to anthropic factors: Tools for an efficient planning. In G.Borruso., S.Bertazzon.,

A.Favretto., B.Murgante., & C.M.Torre. *Geographic information analysis for sustainable development and economic planning: New technologies* (pp. 87–101). IGI Global.

Imbrenda, V., Gómez, C. M., D'Emilio, M., Samela, C., Salvati, L., Matarazzo, N., Lanfredi, M., & Coluzzi, R. (2023). Remote sensing and spatial databases for investigating latent urban-rural dynamics in rural, inland districts of Southern Italy. *Cuadernos de Investigación Geográfica: Geographical Research Letters, 49*(2), 143–162. https://doi.org/10.18172/cig.5806

Imbrenda, V., Maialetti, M., Sateriano, A., Scarpitta, D., Quaranta, G., Chelli, F., & Salvati, L. (2024). Scrutinizing the statistical distribution of a composite index of soil degradation as a measure of early desertification risk in advanced economies. *Environments, 11*(11), 246. https://doi.org/10.3390/environments11110246

IPCC. (2023). *Climate Change 2023: Synthesis Report. Contribution of Working Groups I, II and III to the Sixth Assessment Report of the Intergovernmental Panel on Climate Change* [Core Writing Team, H. Lee and J. Romero (eds.)]. IPCC, Geneva, Switzerland, 184 pp. https://doi.org/10.59327/IPCC/AR6-9789291691647.

Kauffman, N., & Hill, K. (2021). Climate change, adaptation planning and institutional integration: A literature review and framework. *Sustainability, 13*(19), 10708.

Kim, M., You, S., Chon, J., & Lee, J. (2017). Sustainable land-use planning to improve the coastal resilience of the social-ecological landscape. *Sustainability*, *9*(7), 1086.

Kosmas, C., Karamesouti, M., Kounalaki, K., Detsis, V., Vassiliou, P., & Salvati, L. (2016). Land degradation and long-term changes in agro-pastoral systems: An empirical analysis of ecological resilience in Asteroussia - Crete (Greece). *CATENA*, *147*, 196–204. https://doi.org/10.1016/j.catena.2016.07.018

Kourtit, K., Nijkamp, P., & Reid, N. (2014). The new urban world: Challenges and policy. *Applied Geography*, *49*, 1–3.

Lanfredi, M., Coluzzi, R., Imbrenda, V., Nosova, B., Giacalone, M., Turco, R., Prokopovà, M., & Salvati, L. (2023). In-between environmental sustainability and economic viability: An analysis of the state, regulations, and future of Italian forestry sector. *Land*, *12*(5), 1001. https://doi.org/10.3390/land12051001

Lefebvre, M., Espinosa Goded, M., Gomez, Y., & Paloma, S. (2012). The influence of the common agricultural policy on agricultural landscapes. EUR 25459 EN. Publications Office of the European Union, JRC73276.

Li, S., & Li, X. (2017). Global understanding of farmland abandonment: A review and prospects. *Journal of Geographical Sciences*, *27*(9), 1123–1150.

Li, X., Tian, H., Lu, C., & Pan, S. (2023). Four-century history of land transformation by humans in the United States (1630–2020): annual and 1 km grid data for the HIStory of LAND changes (HISLAND-US). *Earth System Science Data*, *15*(2), 1005–1035.

Maialetti, M., Ciaschini, C., Quaranta, G., Salvia, R., Scarpitta, D., Bigiotti, S., Chelli, F. M., & Salvati, L. (2024). Investigating 'land-use trajectories' in Mediterranean rural areas with official statistics and a multiway factor analysis. *Sustainability*, *16*(17), 7644.

Matarazzo, N., Coluzzi, R., Imbrenda, V., Lanfredi, M., Galella, M., & Krauss, D. R. (2025). The role of peripherality in the spread of pandemic: Evidence from Basilicata (Southern Italy) during the first wave of COVID-19. *International Journal of Disaster Risk Reduction*, *122*, 105457.

Meehan, T. D., Werling, B. P., Landis, D. A., & Gratton, C. (2011). Agricultural landscape simplification and insecticide use in the Midwestern United States. *Proceedings of the National Academy of Sciences*, *108*(28), 11500–11505.

Nocentini, S., Buttoud, G., Ciancio, O., & Corona, P. (2017). Managing forests in a changing world: The need for a systemic approach. A review. *Forest Systems*, 26(1), eR01. https://doi.org/10.5424/fs/2017261-09443

OECD. (2025). *Reinforcing rural resilience, OECD rural studies*. OECD Publishing. https://doi.org/10.1787/7cd485e3-en

Oliveira, V. (2016). The study of urban form: Different approaches. In *Urban morphology: An introduction to the study of the physical form of cities* (pp. 87–149). Springer International Publishing.

Pace, L., Imbrenda, V., Lanfredi, M., Cudlín, P., Simoniello, T., Salvati, L., & Coluzzi, R. (2023). Delineating the intrinsic, long-term path of land degradation: A spatially explicit transition matrix for Italy, 1960–2010. *International Journal of Environmental Research and Public Health*, *20*(3), 2402. https://doi.org/10.3390/ijerph20032402

Perrin, C., Nougarèdes, B., Sini, L., Branduini, P., & Salvati, L. (2018). Governance changes in peri-urban farmland protection following decentralisation: A comparison between Montpellier (France) and Rome (Italy). *Land Use Policy*, *70*, 535–546. https://doi.org/10.1016/j.landusepol.2017.09.027

Pricope, N. G., Daldegan, G. A., Zvoleff, A., Mwenda, K. M., Noon, M., & Lopez-Carr, D. (2023). Operationalizing an integrative socio-ecological framework in support of global monitoring of land degradation. *Land Degradation & Development*, *34*(1), 109–124.

Ragosta, M., Daniele, G., Imbrenda, V., Coluzzi, R., D'Emilio, M., Lanfredi, M., & Matarazzo, N. (2024). Land transformations in Irpinia (Southern Italy): A tale on the socio-economic dynamics acting in a marginal area of the Mediterranean Europe. *Sustainability*, *16*(19), 8724. https://doi.org/10.3390/su16198724

Recanatesi, F., Clemente, M., Grigoriadis, E., Ranalli, F., Zitti, M., & Salvati, L. (2015). A fifty-year sustainability assessment of Italian agro-forest districts. *Sustainability*, *8*(1), 32. https://doi.org/10.3390/su8010032

Roldan, C. S., Giraldo, G. A. M., & Santana, E. L. (2023). Sustainable development in rural territories within the last decade: A review of the state of the art. *Heliyon*, *9*(7), 1–12.

Rondeux, J., Bertini, R., Bastrup-Birk, A., Corona, P., Latte, N., McRoberts, R. E., Ståhl, G., Winter, S., & Chirici, G. (2012). Assessing deadwood using harmonized national forest inventory data. *Forest Science*, *58*(3), 269–283. https://doi.org/10.5849/forsci.10-057

Salvati, L., Gemmiti, R., & Perini, L. (2012). Land degradation in Mediterranean urban areas: An unexplored link with planning? *Area*, *44*(3), 317–325. https://doi.org/10.1111/j.1475-4762.2012.01083.x

Salvati, L., Petitta, M., Ceccarelli, T., Perini, L., Di Battista, F., & Scarascia, M. E. V. (2008). Italy's renewable water resources as estimated on the basis of the monthly water balance. *Irrigation and Drainage*, *57*(5), 507–515. https://doi.org/10.1002/ird.380

Salvati, L., & Zitti, M. (2007). Territorial disparities, natural resource distribution, and land degradation: A case study in southern Europe. *GeoJournal*, *70*(2–3), 185–194. https://doi.org/10.1007/s10708-008-9124-1

Salvati, L., & Zitti, M. (2009). Substitutability and weighting of ecological and economic indicators: Exploring the importance of various components of a synthetic index. *Ecological Economics*, *68*(4), 1093–1099. https://doi.org/10.1016/j.ecolecon.2008.07.017

Siddik, M. A., & Islam, A. R. M. T. (2024). Review of coastal land transformation: Factors, impacts, adaptation strategies, and future scopes. *Geography and Sustainability*, *5*(2), 167–178.

Simmie, J., & Martin, R. (2010). The economic resilience of regions: Towards an evolutionary approach. *Cambridge Journal of Regions, Economy and Society*, *3*(1), 27–43.

Turgel, I. D., & Chernova, O. A. (2024). COVID-19 and regional resilience: Trends, priorities, and the geography of research. *Journal of Safety Science and Resilience*, *5*(3), 295–305.

Ustaoglu, E., & Williams, B. (2022). Institutional settings and effects on agricultural land conversion: A global and spatial analysis of European regions. *Land*, *12*(1), 47.

Winkler, K., Fuchs, R., Rounsevell, M., & Herold, M. (2021). Global land use changes are four times greater than previously estimated. *Nature Communications*, *12*(1), 2501.

Zambon, I., Benedetti, A., Ferrara, C., & Salvati, L. (2018). Soil matters? A multivariate analysis of socioeconomic constraints to urban expansion in Mediterranean Europe. *Ecological Economics*, *146*, 173–183. https://doi.org/10.1016/j.ecolecon.2017.10.015

Zambon, I., Colantoni, A., Carlucci, M., Morrow, N., Sateriano, A., & Salvati, L. (2017). Land quality, sustainable development and environmental degradation in agricultural districts: A computational approach based on entropy indexes. *Environmental Impact Assessment Review*, *64*, 37–46. https://doi.org/10.1016/j.eiar.2017.01.003

2

EXPLORING CLIMATE LANDSCAPES: THEORY AND PRACTICES WITH INDICATORS

ALESSIA D'AGATA[a], MARCO MAIALETTI[b], DONATO SCARPITTA[c], IOANNIS KONAXIS[d], ROSA COLUZZI[e], LEONARDO BIANCHINI[f], GIANLUCA EGIDI[f] AND VITO IMBRENDA[e]

[a]*Sapienza University of Rome, Italy*
[b]*Independent Researcher and Lawyer, Italy*
[c]*Independent Researcher and Architect, Italy*
[d]*University of Piraeus, Greece*
[e]*National Research Council of Italy, Institute of Methodologies for Environmental Analysis (CNR-IMAA), Italy*
[f]*University of Tuscia, Italy*

ABSTRACT

The chapter offers a theoretical discussion on the crucial challenge of our millennium: reconciling human development and the capacity of the earth's ecosystems to withstand it. Among the major global causes of natural resource exploitation and irreversible environmental degradation are population growth and agricultural globalization. In this context, forest ecosystems come into play which, if managed rationally, can contribute to mitigating human impact. However, climate change exacerbates the detrimental effects of urbanization, through the alteration of water cycle and water availability. It is therefore urgent to plan resource management policies that limit consumption and regulate withdrawals through spatial planning strategies involving local actors and based on an integrated knowledge of ecological and social peculiarities of the analyzed areas. This approach makes it possible to identify the most vulnerable areas, reduce conflicts, and promote shared actions to safeguard the environment and resources for future generations.

Keywords: Indicators; sustainability; climate change; climatic classification; global warming

INTRODUCTION

The assessment of the magnitude of sustainable human pressure for the Earth's ecosystems still remains one of the major challenges of this millennium (e.g., Salvati & Carlucci, 2014). This quantification should support the design of effective measures to counterbalance the environmental impact of human activities (Meadows et al., 1972). The unsustainable rate of population growth and the widely improved living conditions, even experienced by emerging economies, implied an intense exploitation of ecosystems and a relevant deterioration of natural resources, such as water and soil, as well as energy sources (Rockström et al., 2009). The increase in population has boosted food demand along with the growth in expectations in terms of food quality. This has often implied the substitution of traditional crops with intensive cultivations strictly connected with market globalization (FAO, 2024). This globally recognized phenomenon often results in unsustainable local production structures leading to irreversible processes of environmental degradation throughout time (Castle et al., 2022; Quaranta et al., 2020; Salvati & Carlucci, 2011).

Reconciling the goals of food security and social development still represents a relevant challenge for an increasing global population sharing common rights and responsibilities (Davis et al., 2023). The achievement of these objectives requires to limit ecosystems' alterations and manage the agroforestry sector in an ecologically sound, socially equitable and economically sustainable manner (Imbrenda, Coluzzi, et al., 2023), minimizing the pressure on natural resources to be safeguarded for future generations (Altieri et al., 2018). Agroforestry ecosystems are auto-trophic systems that carry out the biosynthesis of organic matter using solar energy, thereby enabling life on Earth for all organisms, including humans (Colantoni et al., 2015; Plieninger et al., 2020; Salvati et al., 2012).

Agroforestry ecosystems, producing food, fiber, and biomass through the use of solar energy – an inexhaustible and cost-free resource – become indispensable for rebalancing the environmental impact caused by human activities (Davis et al., 2023; Gupta et al., 2023; Lanfredi et al., 2023). In particular, (i) they absorb and metabolize the carbon dioxide released in greater quantities into the atmosphere by human activities; (ii) they absorb atmospheric nitrogen with subsequent synthesis of protein molecules; (iii) they mitigate the risk of extreme climate events and regulate hydrogeological processes; and (iv) they support the preservation of the distinctive character of landscapes.

Anyway, the proper exploitation of ecosystems ensures that their "carrying capacity" is not exceeded, thereby minimizing the environmental impact produced by human activities (Canfora et al., 2017; Ferretti et al., 2014; Pantera et al., 2021). The regular self-renewal of ecosystems is essential for the absorption of pollutants and waste produced by humans, provided their regenerative capacity is not compromised (Forman, 2008). Therefore, agroforestry ecosystems have a multifunctional character since, besides food production, they provide society with a wide range of services and benefits (Ferrara et al., 2017; Francaviglia et al., 2019; Mbow et al., 2014).

The agricultural and forestry sectors become crucial in territorial planning and in designing interventions to restore degraded ecosystems and disrupted natural resource cycles (Jose, 2019). Agriculture, as a human activity, can create imbalances in ecological processes in certain conditions of production intensification (Salvati et al., 2015). In this case, the regime of human interventions should be adjusted to allow agroforestry ecosystems to fulfill their natural role effectively supporting agro-food requirements (Biasi et al., 2019; Gupta et al., 2023; Kosmas et al., 2015).

THE INTRINSIC ROLE OF PLANNING

Ecosystem planning and natural resource management should therefore include interventions caring about the environment and primary production, prioritizing the preservation and protection and, where possible, the improvement of ecosystem quality (Steiner, 2008). At present, awareness of the risks linked to environmental degradation is increasingly widespread and, at the same time, a growing concern raises on the consequences of overexploitation of natural resources (Imbrenda et al., 2013; Tahat et al., 2020; Yang et al., 2024). Current levels of agricultural soil exploitation could soon result in substantial depletion of both water resources and soil fertility, particularly in areas intrinsically susceptible to degradation processes (Davis et al., 2023; Imbrenda, Gómez, et al., 2023; Pace et al., 2023). Soil fertility, strictly connected with agriculture productivity, is seriously threatened by the increasing frequency and intensity of droughts as well as other extreme climatic events (e.g., Incerti et al., 2007). Relying on supplementary irrigation or increasing amounts of fertilizers amplifies the environmental impact of agriculture (Fig. 2.1).

To reconcile the natural environmental balance with socioeconomic development, it is essential to carefully plan the use of natural capital, especially water, in light of the limits and potential of any territory (Castle et al., 2022). Recently, further issues have emerged due to a significant increase in climatic anomalies driven by global warming. A globally recognized climate change characterized by precipitation decrease, temperature increase, and intensification of extreme events, could negatively affect the hydrological cycle in terms of number of inflows and outflows and amount of available water (Quandt et al., 2023). Besides its drastic consequences, this undermines the right of millions of people to access the amount of water needed for their survival and health (Oishy et al., 2025). In more advanced societies, the economic value assigned to water does not perfectly match its true worth, since the market value derived from its use in production processes should be complemented with the value, rather difficult to assess, associated with the maintenance of ecosystems producing the same resource, namely, freshwater (Rahman et al., 2024). This issue often causes enormous resources' wastes within different economic sectors (European Environment Agency, 2021).

Fig. 2.1. Irrigated Tree Crop Systems in Dry Mediterranean Climate.
Source: Authors' Photographic Archive.

The indiscriminate exploitation of water resources, exacerbated by global warming, contributes to significantly higher water consumption than that allowed by the natural hydrological cycle, thereby compromising the future availability of this resource (Calvin et al., 2023). This requires a radical change in water management policies, imposing strict limits on drinking water consumption and serious regulation of withdrawals from surface watercourses and underground aquifers, aimed at mitigating the imbalance between growing demand and decreasing water availability (Postel, 1999). The available water resources of a given territory are determined by the annual flows of its watercourses and aquifers. The total water flow is fed by precipitation which, upon reaching the ground, saturates it and forms surface and underground runoff. A relevant portion of the meteorological inflow from precipitation is returned to the atmosphere through evapotranspiration; the remaining part flows into watercourses, while some is retained as soil moisture, and another fraction percolates through the soil layers, eventually recharging the groundwater aquifers (Oki et al., 2004).

Meteorological factors are therefore the parameters with the greatest weight in the water balance, consequently impacting the renewal of water resources. The unpredictable amount of water resources could be, however, analyzed on the basis of long time series of meteorological data indicating the probability of occurrence of both regular climatic phenomena and extreme events (Nebeker, 1995). Abnormal climate patterns and anthropogenic pressure, as well as improper management of ecosystems and natural resources (such as water and soil), cause alterations to the hydrological cycle (Oki & Kanae, 2006). These are potentially mitigated by the vegetation cover of the agro-forestry-pastoral ecosystems. They affect the distribution of inflows and outflows and the speed and amount of surface runoff during heavy rainfall, promoting the infiltration of rainwater into the soil and aquifer recharge, reducing soil erosion, counteracting slope instability, and thus mitigating the impact of extreme weather events (Lin, 2010). Anyway, the bulk of complex issues related to land-use planning are further exacerbated by the excessive number of public institutions ideally collaborating to address environmental problems (Christou et al., 1999).

The activities proposed by the various bodies entrusted by law with territorial planning and the programming of strategies to be implemented should be coordinated in parallel, avoiding harmful overlaps (Desta et al., 2021). This scenario requires effective coordination among all bodies responsible for land-use management and conservation of natural resources. These organizations should operate within a comprehensive framework spending commitments, promoting not only economically convenient solutions, rather offering clear and lasting benefits across all sectors. Effective policies should be required to avoid the relevant socioeconomic burden connected to the detrimental consequences of environmental degradation, caused by improper land management (Abu Hammad & Tumeizi, 2012).

A comprehensive approach, based on the ecological characteristics of the territory, allows for a synoptic reading at various spatial and temporal scales, to acquire objective information on the different levels of vulnerability of the areas aimed at designing shared strategies for the restoration of territories (Berry et al., 2006). This document proposes an investigation scheme, suitable for future in-depth studies within other fields of study, to be developed through progressive levels of greater detail, both in terms of spatial and temporal resolutions. The reduction in usable water flow, combined with the increase in consumption recorded in all sectors, leads to the prediction of numerous water crises that can quickly lead to disastrous consequences (Fig. 2.2).

Such crises should be avoided by reducing waste and increasing efficiency in use of water reserves through appropriate hydraulic works. Water availability and quality crucially affect the survival of all living organisms and, in

Fig. 2.2. Dry Agricultural Landscapes Exploiting Extensive Crops and Exposed to Increasing Drought Risk in Southern Europe.
Source: Authors' Photographic Archive.

turn, of agroforestry ecosystems, whose stability and proper functioning support the whole agrifood system. The environmental impact on land systems from human pressure can be assessed by comparing the proportion of land devoted to plant ecosystems with population density.

A territorial analysis that highlights the relationship between society and natural resources can enable the design of policy measures to mediate between the interests of the various actors involved through the use of methodologies capable of providing operational tools to (i) develop a territorial knowledge base; (ii) process the collected data to be aggregated into summary indexes; (iii) highlight the dynamics of natural processes and the risks resulting from their alteration; (iv) identify the decision-making tools for intervention to be communicated to the institutions involved.

Considering the results of the analysis and the strong interrelationships between rural population, territory, and environmental impact, the work assesses the degree of environmental vulnerability of different areas to determine the suitability of strategies to be implemented according to land use and multiple environmental factors. Subsequently, all interacting components can be reorganized to provide a unified vision of the territory, ensuring an appropriate balance between natural resources and their users (Salvati & Zitti, 2009).

Territorial reorganization and the rational management of resources should therefore be planned with the aim of protecting the environment and its natural and social components, while assessing, on a case-by-case basis and through the estimation of human pressure, the degree of urgency and priority of potential interventions. The planned actions should lead to the reorganization of economic activities based on the type of relationship between population and landscape (Ragosta et al., 2024) with the involvement of all stakeholders, to share resource management choices and responsibilities. A simultaneous cooperation between the relevant public institutions allows for agreed decisions on the incentives to be provided, through peaceful negotiation to avoid new conflicts and resolve the existing ones.

CLIMATE MONITORING

Climate can be defined as the set of atmospheric conditions characterized by the stages and evolution of the weather in each area, according to the World Meteorological Organization (WMO). Climate is one of the most relevant factors determining the biotic components of ecosystems, whether natural or artificial (Trewartha et al., 1980). This relevance is associated with its discriminating action on the life of plants and animals and with the conditioning action (exerted at the pedogenetic level) on the chemical-physical structure of the soil and on the relative water availability.

By defining a scale representing a specific territorial coverage, with regard to climate, it is possible to distinguish and identify macro-climate, meso-climate, and micro-climate regimes (Barry & Chorley, 2009). The macro-climate manifests itself in a large territory, in rather strict dependence on geographical factors such as latitude, longitude, and distance from the sea; an example of an investigation scale could be the area of the Mediterranean basin. As for the meso-climate, it concerns the variations that the macro-climate undergoes at the regional level, especially in relation with local geo-topographical conditions. Finally, the micro-climate can be defined as the climate that manifests itself in a restricted, point-like area, for instance in the undergrowth of a forest. In climatology, the main considered factors include solar radiation (quantified through duration of sunshine and the quantity of radiation), air temperature, atmospheric pressure, air humidity and precipitation. These factors have been affected by geographical features, such as the distribution of land and sea, air masses and circulation models, mountain systems, internal lakes and vegetation cover (Fig. 2.3), able to determine variations in local climate conditions (Calvin et al., 2023).

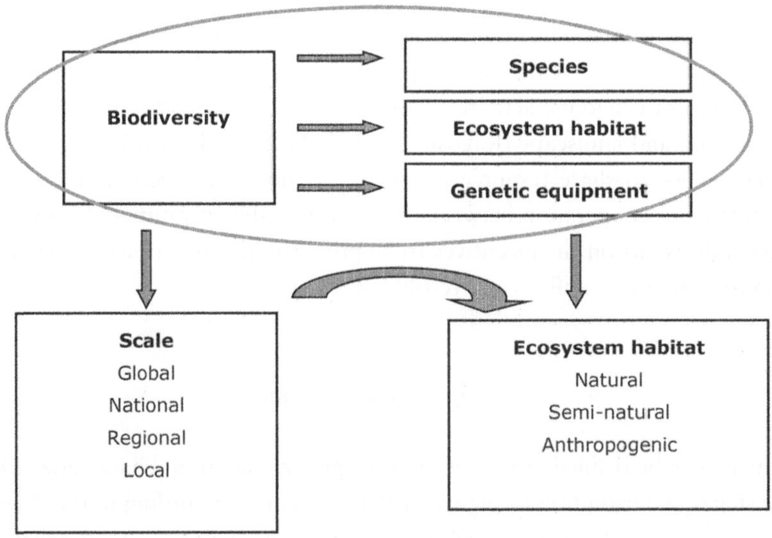

Fig. 2.3. Schematic Example of the Functioning and Interactions Existing in an Ecosystem at Various Geographical Scales.
Source: Authors' Elaboration of Recent Literature.

Variables and Indicators

Weather characteristics or variables are easily measurable physical quantities affected by climatic factors. The most significant ones for the development of climatic indices are rainfall and temperature. The geographical distribution of temperature can be represented cartographically through isotherms, or lines connecting locations with the same measured temperature values. Isotherms always tend to form concentric surfaces surrounding mountainous reliefs. The development of such maps can be useful for (direct and immediate) identification of correlation regimes between the distribution of certain agricultural (or ecologically) relevant species and the spatial trend of isotherms. A further element for defining climatic indices is the amount of precipitation over a given time window.

Generally, precipitation can have different natures and origins (in fact, orographic, convective, cyclonic rains can be distinguished); however, precipitation can generally be described as the result of water vapor reaching atmospheric concentrations that exceed saturation, or due to a significant reduction in air temperature that causes condensation. In this way, precipitation in the form of rain, snow, or hail is generated. Similarly to what happens with temperatures, the daily measurement is taken as a reference also for precipitation, and subsequently the quantities can be calculated on a monthly and yearly basis (European Environment Agency, 2021). Moreover, for the variable precipitation, geographical distribution maps can be constructed, the so-called isohyets where the lines connect points on the Earth's surface with the same annual or month rainfall amounts. Temperature and precipitation are elements used by the most well-known climate indices and are particularly useful for defining a characteristic climate category (FAO, 2024).

Climatic Types

The distinction of climate types represents a form of taxonomy or classification; each clearly identified class corresponds to a typical land cover (De Castro et al., 2007). The distribution of species within certain areas and, consequently, the definition of characteristic areas, may not depend exclusively on climatic factors and elements, but also on territorial, historical, and anthropogenic factors (Reyes-García et al., 2016). Several indices have been proposed to classify the different climate typologies observed worldwide. Among the others, it is worth mentioning the following approaches:

1) Lang's "pluviofactor," represented by the ratio *P/T* (*P* represents the annual precipitation expressed in cm and *T* represents the average

annual temperature expressed in °C). According to this index, for instance, the limit between arboreal and steppe vegetation corresponds to pluviofactor values lower than 1; instead, for pluviofactor values lower than 0.5, there is a transition to desert ecosystems.

2) De Martonne aridity index slightly modifies Lang's formula to avoid values that are too large or negative in the case of cold climates and the annual mean T is less than or equal to 0. In this way, the index takes the form: $I = P/T + 10$ (P represents the annual precipitation expressed in mm and T represents the annual mean temperature expressed in °C). The two indices are characterized by an analogous environmental relevance. For values below 5, desert vegetation prevails; for values between 5 and 10, steppe vegetation; for values between 10 and 20, grassland vegetation; and, for values, above 20, forest vegetation.

3) Kira thermal index (WI, Warmth index, total heat available for plant growth) with WI = sum $(t - 5)$ (where t = average month temperatures above 5 °C).

4) Rivas-Martinez Index, determines the thermo-type through the formula $(T + m + M) \times 10$ (T represents the average annual temperature, m represents the average minimum temperature of the coldest month, and M represents the average maximum temperature of the coldest month). This index, mainly relying on temperature and rainfall, allows for the evaluation of both the intensity of the winter cold and the annual thermal amplitude. The ombrotype results from the sum of the precipitation of those months showing an average temperature above 0 °C divided by the sum of the average temperatures in the same months.

Graphical Representation

In addition to climate indices, graphical representation methods of the essential climate variables, in a system of Cartesian axes, are also very effective. In this sense, reference is made to climograms, i.e., precise graphical representations of the climate that allow for an immediate comparison between the regimes of different locations. These are graphs that show the months of the year on the x-axis and the average monthly temperatures and precipitation on the y-axis with a ratio of 1:2 between the P scale and the T scale. When the temperature rises above the precipitation curve, climate aridity occurs. Obviously, the greater the overlap, the higher the resulting level of aridity (Fig. 2.4). Climate indices are crucial to develop phyto-climatic maps of a given territory, allowing

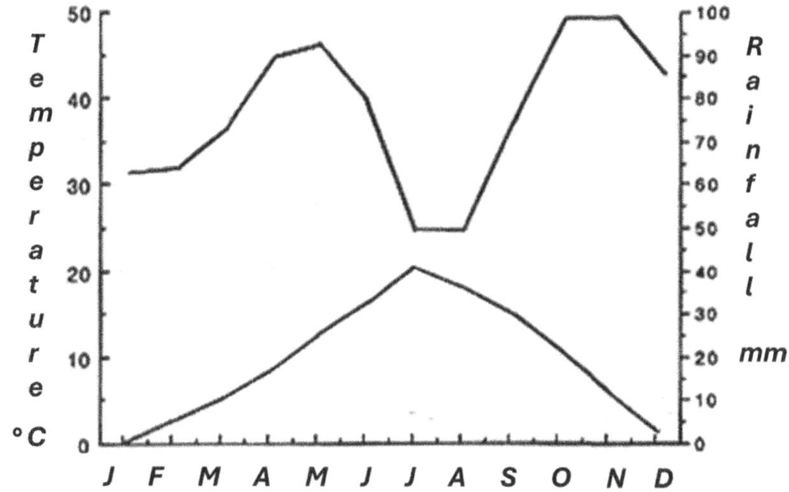

Fig. 2.4. An Example of Rivas-Martinez Diagram Illustrating Average Air Temperature and Rainfall by Month in a Given Place.
Source: Authors' Adaptation of Recent Literature.

the identification of potential vegetation with a high degree of accuracy. The resulting cartography, in turn, becomes a fundamental tool for examining the dynamism that characterizes the vegetation of a given area and for designing suitable resource policies.

The Role of Bio-indicators

The survival, development, and reproductive capacity of living beings are closely connected to the environments in which they live. This close connection justifies the widespread use of "bio-indicators," i.e., animals and especially plants (due to their immobility) taken as "environmental sentinels" (Blasi et al., 2014) investigating ecosystems and their climatic conditions, and carefully monitoring pollutants (Peel et al., 2007). Among the organisms capable of providing a complete bio-monitoring of air pollution, epiphytic lichens (i.e., lichens that grow on tree trunks) occupy a prominent position because they can be used both as bio-indicators and as bio-accumulators. Lichens could absorb and accumulate harmful elements and contaminants present in the atmosphere; this allows the analysis of the bioaccumulation (i.e., concentration and degree of diffusion) of various pollutants such as heavy metals, chlorinated hydrocarbons, and radio nuclides. The method for detecting air pollution using epiphytic lichens is based on the abundance of lichen species, also associated with the average climate conditions of the investigated area. The biodiversity values are interpreted in terms of departure from the expected naturalness, determined by pollutants causing the decrease of lichen communities in terms of species number and their coverage/frequency. Lichens are, indeed, able to react relatively quickly to deterioration of air quality and can recolonize urban and industrial environments with improved ecological conditions in just a few years, as observed in many parts of Europe. The measure of lichen biodiversity is defined as the sum of the frequencies of lichen species in a survey grid of fixed dimensions. Moreover, the optimal visualization of the detected environmental conditions can be achieved through a cartographic elaboration showing the classification of the investigated area in zones with different lichen biodiversity: each naturalness/alteration class is associated with a different color (Table 2.1).

The presence of certain species in each environment or, more precisely, the floristic composition of a given environment, is not a random phenomenon. On the contrary, it should be strictly correlated to the presence of certain environmental conditions, which can satisfy the "ecological niche" needs of each individual floristic element. Each species, being associated with a characteristic adaptive range with respect to environmental factors (for instance, the presence of mineral salts in the soil, temperature, humidity), acts as a bio-indicator, highlighting visible effects at a macroscopic level (in terms of bearing, appearance) or simply through its presence–absence. Plant indicators therefore provide a good description, through their adaptive plasticity related to micro- and macro-environmental conditions, of the intensity, extent, and duration of a certain phenomenon causing specific effects, which can generate a disturbance (Han et al., 2025). The concept of "disturbance" should be

Table 2.1. Scale of Naturalness Taken from the "Guidelines for Bio-monitoring with Epiphytic Lichens."

British Lichen Society (BLS) value	Rating	Color
>50	very high naturalness	Blue
41–50	high naturalness	Dark green
31–40	medium naturalness	Light green
21–30	low naturalness/low impairment	Yellow
11–20	average alteration	Orange
01–10	high alteration	Red
0	very high alteration	Brown

Source: Our Adaptation of Nimis (1999) Data.

understood as a situation that deviates from the conditions within the range of adaptation and from the optimal value with respect to certain ecological factors (e.g., Fares et al., 2017). Ultimately, it is important to emphasize that climate significantly affects the balance of life not only in natural ecosystems but also in anthropogenic ecosystems, such as agricultural ones.

CONCLUDING REMARKS

The information obtained from accurate statistical analysis of a historical series of meteorological data and census data allows outlining a general picture of the current ecological conditions and the ongoing variations of some of their components (Sallustio et al., 2018). The general trend observed in many regions of the Earth, toward rising temperatures, decreasing rainfall, and increased seasonal asymmetry (Lanfredi et al., 2020), can impact agroforestry ecosystems hindering their ability to provide goods and services. Temperature increase and rainfall reduction can cause alterations in the water cycle and the physiological processes of ecosystems (Salvati et al., 2013).

As a direct consequence, there is a reduced synthesis of biomass in forests and winter crops, and a greater demand for irrigation water for spring-summer cycle crops (Begon & Townsend, 2021). Climate change also negatively influences the hydrological balance with deleterious effects on the regeneration of water resources in a given area. Climate change also causes a progressive expansion of degraded areas worldwide, affecting both economically advanced regions and developing countries (Carlucci et al., 2022). Knowledge of the climate and its potential variations is a factor that should be considered, directly or indirectly, when planning agricultural activities (Canfora et al., 2017).

The term "climate variability" indicates the natural climate variability that has always been observed over time and which is just an environmental feature (Dore, 2005; Hulme et al., 1999; Salinger, 2005). On the other hand, the term "climate change" currently indicates a variability induced by human actions that force natural variability (Troccoli et al., 2015). The assessment of the relationship between climate change, agriculture, and ecosystems in a given region could not prescind from analyzing temperature and precipitation trends over the last few decades, water availability in agricultural land, and intense precipitation recorded in a certain area (Seifollahi-Aghmiuni et al., 2022). As far as purely agricultural aspects are concerned, the lack of rain severely damages the natural fertility and productivity of the soil and, over time, compromises the achievement of good results from sustainable agricultural practices.

REFERENCES

Abu Hammad, A., & Tumeizi, A. (2012). Land degradation: Socioeconomic and environmental causes and consequences in the eastern Mediterranean. *Land Degradation & Development*, *23*(3), 216–226. https://doi.org/10.1002/ldr.1069

Altieri, M. A., Farrell, J. G., Hecht, S. B., Liebman, M., Magdoff, F., Murphy, B., Norgaard, R. B., & Sikor, T. O. (2018). *Agroecology: The science of sustainable agriculture* (2° ed.). CRC Press. https://doi.org/10.1201/9780429495465

Barry, R. G., & Chorley, R. J. (2009). *Atmosphere, weather and climate.* Routledge. https://doi.org/10.4324/9780203871027

Begon, M., & Townsend, C. R. (2021). *Ecology: From individuals to ecosystems* (5° ed.). Wiley.

Berry, P. M., Rounsevell, M. D., Harrison, P. A., & Audsley, E. (2006). Assessing the vulnerability of agricultural land use and species to climate change and the role of policy in facilitating adaptation. *Environmental Science & Policy*, *9*(2), 189–204.

Biasi, R., Brunori, E., Ferrara, C., & Salvati, L. (2019). Assessing impacts of climate change on phenology and quality traits of Vitis vinifera L.: The contribution of local knowledge. *Plants*, *8*(5), 121.

Blasi, C., Capotorti, G., Copiz, R., Guida, D., Mollo, B., Smiraglia, D., & Zavattero, L. (2014). Classification and mapping of the ecoregions of Italy. *Plant Biosystems - An International Journal Dealing with All Aspects of Plant Biology*, *148*(6), 1255–1345. https://doi.org/10.1080/11263504.2014.985756

Calvin, K., Dasgupta, D., Krinner, G., Mukherji, A., Thorne, P. W., Trisos, C., Romero, J., Aldunce, P., Barrett, K., Blanco, G., Cheung, W. W. L., Connors, S., Denton, F., Diongue-Niang, A., Dodman, D., Garschagen, M., Geden, O., Hayward, B., Jones, C., & Péan, C. (2023). *IPCC, 2023: Climate Change 2023: Synthesis Report. Contribution of Working Groups I, II and III to the Sixth Assessment Report of the Intergovernmental Panel on Climate Change* [Core Writing Team, H. Lee and J. Romero (eds.)]. IPCC, Geneva, Switzerland. (First). Intergovernmental Panel on Climate Change (IPCC). https://doi.org/10.59327/IPCC/AR6-9789291691647.

Canfora, L., Salvati, L., Benedetti, A., & Francaviglia, R. (2017). Is soil microbial diversity affected by soil and groundwater salinity? Evidences from a coastal system in central Italy. *Environmental Monitoring and Assessment*, *189*, 1–15.

Carlucci, M., Salvia, R., Quaranta, G., Salvati, L., & Imbrenda, V. (2022). Official statistics, spatio-temporal dynamics and local-scale monitoring: Toward integrated environmental-economic accounting for land degradation. *Letters in Spatial and Resource Sciences*, *15*(3), 469–491. https://doi.org/10.1007/s12076-022-00319-y

Castle, S. E., Miller, D. C., Merten, N., Ordonez, P. J., & Baylis, K. (2022). Evidence for the impacts of agroforestry on ecosystem services and human well-being in high-income countries: A systematic map. *Environmental Evidence*, *11*(1), 10. https://doi.org/10.1186/s13750-022-00260-4

Christou, M. D., Amendola, A., & Smeder, M. (1999). The control of major accident hazards: The land-use planning issue. *Journal of Hazardous Materials*, *65*(1–2), 151–178. https://doi.org/10.1016/S0304-3894(98)00261-1

Colantoni, A., Ferrara, C., Perini, L., & Salvati, L. (2015). Assessing trends in climate aridity and vulnerability to soil degradation in Italy. *Ecological Indicators*, *48*, 599–604.

Davis, A. G., Huggins, D. R., & Reganold, J. P. (2023). Linking soil health and ecological resilience to achieve agricultural sustainability. *Frontiers in Ecology and the Environment*, *21*(3), 131–139. https://doi.org/10.1002/fee.2594

De Castro, M., Gallardo, C., Jylha, K., & Tuomenvirta, H. (2007). The use of a climate-type classification for assessing climate change effects in Europe from an ensemble of nine regional climate models. *Climatic Change*, *81*(S1), 329–341. https://doi.org/10.1007/s10584-006-9224-1

Desta, G., Tamene, L., Abera, W., Amede, T., & Whitbread, A. (2021). Effects of land management practices and land cover types on soil loss and crop productivity in Ethiopia: A review. *International Soil and Water Conservation Research*, *9*(4), 544–554. https://doi.org/10.1016/j.iswcr.2021.04.008

Dore, M. H. (2005). Climate change and changes in global precipitation patterns: What do we know? *Environment International*, *31*(8), 1167–1181.

European Environment Agency. (2021). *Water resources across Europe: Confronting water stress: an updated assessment*. Publications Office of the European Union. https://doi.org/10.2800/320975

FAO. (2024). *The State of Food and Agriculture 2024*. FAO. https://doi.org/10.4060/cd2616en

Fares, S., Bajocco, S., Salvati, L., Camarretta, N., Dupuy, J.-L., Xanthopoulos, G., Guijarro, M., Madrigal, J., Hernando, C., & Corona, P. (2017). Characterizing potential wildland fire fuel in live vegetation in the Mediterranean region. *Annals of Forest Science*, *74*, 1–14.

Ferrara, C., Carlucci, M., Grigoriadis, E., Corona, P., & Salvati, L. (2017). A comprehensive insight into the geography of forest cover in Italy: Exploring the importance of socioeconomic local contexts. *Forest Policy and Economics*, *75*, 12–22.

Ferretti, M., Marchetto, A., Arisci, S., Bussotti, F., Calderisi, M., Carnicelli, S., Cecchini, G.; Fabbio, G., Bertini, G., Matteucci, G., de Cinti, B., Salvati, L., & Pompei, E. (2014). On the tracks of Nitrogen deposition effects on temperate forests at their southern European range–an observational study from Italy. *Global Change Biology*, *20*(11), 3423–3438.

Forman, R. T. T. (2008). *Land mosaics: The ecology of landscapes and regions* (9. print., transferred to digital printing). Cambridge Univ. Press.

Francaviglia, R., Di Bene, C., Farina, R., Salvati, L., & Vicente-Vicente, J. L. (2019). Assessing "4 per 1000" soil organic carbon storage rates under Mediterranean climate: A comprehensive data analysis. *Mitigation and Adaptation Strategies for Global Change*, *24*, 795–818.

Gupta, S. R., Dagar, J. C., Sileshi, G. W., & Chaturvedi, R. K. (2023). Agroforestry for climate change resilience in degraded landscapes. In J. C. Dagar, S. R. Gupta, & G. W. Sileshi (Eds.), *Agroforestry for Sustainable Intensification of Agriculture in Asia and Africa* (pp. 121–174). Springer Nature Singapore. https://doi.org/10.1007/978-981-19-4602-8_5

Han, J., Michell, J., & Umstead, M. (2025). Charge-dipole-dipole interactions in cold gases. *Academia Quantum*, *2*(1). https://doi.org/10.20935/AcadQuant7552

Hulme, M., Barrow, E. M., Arnell, N. W., Harrison, P. A., Johns, T. C., & Downing, T. E. (1999). Relative impacts of human-induced climate change and natural climate variability. *Nature*, *397*(6721), 688–691.

Imbrenda, V., Coluzzi, R., Mariani, F., Nosova, B., Cudlinova, E., Salvia, R., Quaranta, G., Salvati, L., & Lanfredi, M. (2023). Working in (slow) progress: Socio-environmental and economic dynamics in the forestry sector and the contribution to sustainable development in Europe. *Sustainability*, *15*(13), 10271. https://doi.org/10.3390/su151310271

Imbrenda, V., D'Emilio, M., Lanfredi, M., Ragosta, M., & Simoniello, T. (2013). Indicators of land degradation vulnerability due to anthropic factors: Tools for an efficient planning. In *Geographic information analysis for sustainable development and economic planning: New technologies* (pp. 87–101). IGI Global.

Imbrenda, V., Gómez, C. M., D'Emilio, M., Samela, C., Salvati, L., Matarazzo, N., Lanfredi, M., & Coluzzi, R. (2023). Remote sensing and spatial databases for investigating latent urban-rural dynamics in rural, inland districts of Southern Italy. *Cuadernos de Investigación Geográfica: Geographical Research Letters*, *49*(2), 143–162. https://doi.org/10.18172/cig.5806

Incerti, G., Feoli, E., Salvati, L., Brunetti, A., & Giovacchini, A. (2007). Analysis of bioclimatic time series and their neural network-based classification to characterise drought risk patterns in South Italy. *International Journal of Biometeorology*, *51*, 253–263.

Jose, S. (2019). Environmental impacts and benefits of agroforestry. In S. Jose (Ed.), *Oxford research encyclopedia of environmental science*. Oxford University Press. https://doi.org/10.1093/acrefore/9780199389414.013.195

Kosmas, C., Detsis, V., Karamesouti, M., Kounalaki, K., Vassiliou, P., & Salvati, L. (2015). Exploring long-term impact of grazing management on land degradation in the socio-ecological system of Asteroussia Mountains, Greece. *Land*, *4*(3), 541–559.

Lanfredi, M., Coluzzi, R., Imbrenda, V., Macchiato, M., & Simoniello, T. (2020). Analyzing space–time coherence in precipitation seasonality across different European climates. *Remote Sensing*, *12*(1), 171. https://doi.org/10.3390/rs12010171

Lanfredi, M., Coluzzi, R., Imbrenda, V., Nosova, B., Giacalone, M., Turco, R., Prokopovà, M., & Salvati, L. (2023). In-between environmental sustainability and economic viability: An analysis of the state, regulations, and future of Italian forestry sector. *Land*, *12*(5), 1001. https://doi.org/10.3390/land12051001

Lin, B. B. (2010). The role of agroforestry in reducing water loss through soil evaporation and crop transpiration in coffee agroecosystems. *Agricultural and Forest Meteorology*, *150*(4), 510–518. https://doi.org/10.1016/j.agrformet.2009.11.010

Mbow, C., Van Noordwijk, M., Luedeling, E., Neufeldt, H., Minang, P. A., & Kowero, G. (2014). Agroforestry solutions to address food security and climate change challenges in Africa. *Current Opinion in Environmental Sustainability*, 6, 61–67. https://doi.org/10.1016/j.cosust.2013.10.014

Meadows, D. H., Meadows, D. L., Randers, J., & Behrens, W. W. (1972). *The limits to growth: A report for the Club of Rome's project on the predicament of mankind*. Universe Books. https://doi.org/10.1349/ddlp.1

Nebeker, F. (1995). *Calculating the weather: Meteorology in the 20th century*. Academic Press.

Nimis, P. (1999). Linee guida per la bioindicazione degli effetti dell'inquinamento tramite la biodiversità dei licheni epifiti. *Agenzia Nazionale per la Protezione dell'Ambiente* (ANPA), Rome, Italy.

Oishy, M. N., Shemonty, N. A., Fatema, S. I., Mahbub, S., Mim, E. L., Hasan Raisa, M. B., & Anik, A. H. (2025). Unravelling the effects of climate change on the soil-plant-atmosphere interactions: A critical review. *Soil & Environmental Health*, *3*(1), 100130. https://doi.org/10.1016/j.seh.2025.100130

Oki, T., Entekhabi, D., & Harrold, T. I. (2004). The global water cycle. In R. S. J. Sparks & C. J. Hawkesworth (A c. Di), *Geophysical Monograph Series* (Vol. 150, pp. 225–237). American Geophysical Union. https://doi.org/10.1029/150GM18

Oki, T., & Kanae, S. (2006). Global hydrological cycles and world water resources. *Science*, *313*(5790), 1068–1072. https://doi.org/10.1126/science.1128845

Pace, L., Imbrenda, V., Lanfredi, M., Cudlín, P., Simoniello, T., Salvati, L., & Coluzzi, R. (2023). Delineating the intrinsic, long-term path of land degradation: A spatially explicit transition matrix for Italy, 1960–2010. *International Journal of Environmental Research and Public Health*, *20*(3), 2402.

Pantera, A., Mosquera-Losada, M. R., Herzog, F., & Den Herder, M. (2021). Agroforestry and the environment. *Agroforestry Systems*, *95*(5), 767–774. https://doi.org/10.1007/s10457-021-00640-8

Peel, M. C., Finlayson, B. L., & McMahon, T. A. (2007). Updated world map of the Köppen-Geiger climate classification. *Hydrology and Earth System Sciences*, *11*(5), 1633–1644. https://doi.org/10.5194/hess-11-1633-2007

Plieninger, T., Muñoz-Rojas, J., Buck, L. E., & Scherr, S. J. (2020). Agroforestry for sustainable landscape management. *Sustainability Science*, *15*(5), 1255–1266. https://doi.org/10.1007/s11625-020-00836-4

Postel, S. (1999). *Pillar of sand: Can the irrigation miracle last?* Norton.

Quandt, A., Neufeldt, H., & Gorman, K. (2023). Climate change adaptation through agroforestry: Opportunities and gaps. *Current Opinion in Environmental Sustainability*, *60*, 101244. https://doi.org/10.1016/j.cosust.2022.101244

Quaranta, G., Salvia, R., Salvati, L., Paola, V. D., Coluzzi, R., Imbrenda, V., & Simoniello, T. (2020). Long-term impacts of grazing management on land degradation in a rural community of Southern Italy: Depopulation matters. *Land Degradation & Development*, *31*(16), 2379–2394.

Ragosta, M., Daniele, G., Imbrenda, V., Coluzzi, R., D'Emilio, M., Lanfredi, M., & Matarazzo, N. (2024). Land transformations in Irpinia (Southern Italy): A tale on the socio-economic dynamics acting in a marginal area of the Mediterranean Europe. *Sustainability*, *16*(19), 8724. https://doi.org/10.3390/su16198724

Rahman, Md. M., Biswas, J. C., & Meena, R. S. (A c. Di). (2024). *Climate change and soil-water-plant nexus: Agriculture and environment*. Springer Nature Singapore. https://doi.org/10.1007/978-981-97-6635-2

Reyes-García, V., Fernández-Llamazares, Á., Guèze, M., Garcés, A., Mallo, M., Vila-Gómez, M., & Vilaseca, M. (2016). Local indicators of climate change: The potential contribution of local knowledge to climate research. *WIREs Climate Change*, 7(1), 109–124. https://doi.org/10.1002/wcc.374

Rockström, J., Steffen, W., Noone, K., Persson, Å., Chapin, F. S., Lambin, E. F., Lenton, T. M., Scheffer, M., Folke, C., Schellnhuber, H. J., Nykvist, B., De Wit, C. A., Hughes, T., Van Der Leeuw, S., Rodhe, H., Sörlin, S., Snyder, P. K., Costanza, R., Svedin, U., & Foley, J. A. (2009). A safe operating space for humanity. *Nature*, *461*(7263), 472–475. https://doi.org/10.1038/461472a

Salinger, M. J. (2005). Climate variability and change: Past, present and future–an overview. *Climatic Change*, *70*(1), 9–29.

Sallustio, L., Pettenella, D., Merlini, P., Romano, R., Salvati, L., Marchetti, M., & Corona, P. (2018). Assessing the economic marginality of agricultural lands in Italy to support land use planning. *Land Use Policy*, *76*, 526–534.

Salvati, L., & Carlucci, M. (2011). The economic and environmental performances of rural districts in Italy: Are competitiveness and sustainability compatible targets? *Ecological Economics*, *70*(12), 2446–2453.

Salvati, L., & Carlucci, M. (2014). A composite index of sustainable development at the local scale: Italy as a case study. *Ecological Indicators*, *43*, 162–171.

Salvati, L., & Zitti, M. (2009). Substitutability and weighting of ecological and economic indicators: Exploring the importance of various components of a synthetic index. *Ecological Economics*, *68*(4), 1093–1099.

Salvati, L., Mavrakis, A., Colantoni, A., Mancino, G., & Ferrara, A. (2015). Complex adaptive systems, soil degradation and land sensitivity to desertification: A multivariate assessment of Italian agro-forest landscape. *Science of the Total Environment*, *521*, 235–245.

Salvati, L., Perini, L., Sabbi, A., & Bajocco, S. (2012). Climate aridity and land use changes: A regional-scale analysis. *Geographical Research*, *50*(2), 193–203.

Salvati, L., Tombolini, I., Perini, L., & Ferrara, A. (2013). Landscape changes and environmental quality: the evolution of land vulnerability and potential resilience to degradation in Italy. *Regional Environmental Change*, *13*, 1223–1233.

Seifollahi-Aghmiuni, S., Kalantari, Z., Egidi, G., Gaburova, L., & Salvati, L. (2022). Urbanisation-driven land degradation and socioeconomic challenges in peri-urban areas: Insights from Southern Europe. *Ambio*, *51*(6), 1446–1458.

Steiner, F. R. (2008). *The living landscape, second edition: An ecological approach to landscape planning* (2nd ed.). Island Press.

Tahat, M., M. Alananbeh, K., A. Othman, Y., & Leskovar, D. (2020). Soil health and sustainable agriculture. *Sustainability*, *12*(12), 4859. https://doi.org/10.3390/su12124859

Trewartha, G. T., Horn, L. H., & Trewartha, G. T. (1980). *An introduction to climate* (5th ed.). McGraw-Hill.

Troccoli, A., Maddaluno, C., Mucci, M., Russo, M., & Rinaldi, M. (2015). Is it appropriate to support the farmers for adopting conservation agriculture? Economic and environmental impact assessment. *Italian Journal of Agronomy*, *10*(4), 661.

Yang, Y., Tilman, D., Jin, Z., Smith, P., Barrett, C. B., Zhu, Y.-G., Burney, J., D'Odorico, P., Fantke, P., Fargione, J., Finlay, J. C., Rulli, M. C., Sloat, L., Jan Van Groenigen, K., West, P. C., Ziska, L., Michalak, A. M., the Clim-Ag Team, Lobell, D. B., & Zhuang, M. (2024). Climate change exacerbates the environmental impacts of agriculture. *Science*, *385*(6713), eadn3747. https://doi.org/10.1126/science.adn3747

3

SOIL ARIDITY, AGRICULTURE, AND CLIMATE WARMING

ALESSIA D'AGATA[a], MARCO MAIALETTI[b], ADELE SATERIANO[c], JESUS RODRIGO COMINO[d], CATERINA SAMELA[e], TIZIANA SIMONIELLO[e], LETIZIA PACE[f] AND MARIA LANFREDI[e]

[a]Sapienza University of Rome, Italy
[b]Independent Researcher and Lawyer, Italy
[c]Mediterranean Sustainable Development Foundation (MEDES), Italy
[d]Universidad de Granada, Spain
[e]National Research Council of Italy, Institute of Methodologies for Environmental Analysis (CNR-IMAA), Italy
[f]University of Bari Aldo Moro, Italy

ABSTRACT

The present contribution performs a joint analysis of temperature regimes and rainfall to assess the impact of climate and soil aridity on ecologically fragile agricultural systems in Italy. It relies on the empirical results derived from quantitative elaboration of meteorological time series at both national and regional levels. To this purpose, soil Aridity Index (AI) provided by the United Nations Environment Programme (UNEP) has been adopted to analyze trends in climate aridity. Throughout the time period analyzed, especially in the latest years, the progressive reduction in rainfall combined with increasing temperatures contributed to further worsening the imbalance between rainfall amount and agricultural water requirements.

Keywords: Climate variations; soil; agriculture; Mediterranean region; water balance

INTRODUCTION

The present study relies on detailed territorial data sources providing estimates of the main climatic and meteorological variables at different levels of spatial aggregation, such as agricultural districts and land reclamation consortia. It aims at integrating official statistics with more accurately assessed sustainable development aspects related to climate change over the past century (Biasi et al., 2019; Incerti et al., 2007; Salvati et al., 2008). Besides climate data, results complement official statistics on national hydrological frameworks informing on the flow of major watercourses (e.g., flow rates and hydrometric heights) to develop indicators for assessing water resources and estimating the components of the hydrological balance at the river basin level (Allen, 2000).

Throughout the last years, Mediterranean Europe – and particularly Italy – was facing key ecological challenges in terms of water availability, particularly in connection with the increased climatic variability and ineffective practices of management of soil and water resources (Brunetti et al., 2006a; Francaviglia et al., 2019; Kosmas et al., 2015). Within the debate on the causes and design of more suitable interventions, scholars observed a progressive global warming also affecting the territorial distribution of rainfalls (Dore, 2005; Luppichini et al., 2022; Molinié et al., 2012). For Mediterranean countries, climate projections have highlighted a general reduction in water availability, connected to scarce and irregular rainfalls, and characterized by short terms more intense events, compared with the observed historical trends (Berdugo et al., 2020; Brunetti et al., 2006b, 2006c; Lanfredi et al., 2020).

The peculiar territorial configuration of Italy generates a marked heterogeneity between climatic regimes, also reflected in the local hydro-meteorological dynamics (Salvati et al., 2015). As a consequence, trends in temperature and rainfalls show significant territorial variations connected both to the structural component of climate and the intrinsic variability of the weather (Fratianni & Acquaotta, 2017; Huang et al., 2017; Messeri et al., 2015).

Among the main drawbacks of climate change within the Mediterranean contexts, an increase in the frequency of drought episodes has been observed along with an intensification of climate aridity, with relevant impacts on agro-forest systems (Colantoni et al., 2015; Lickley & Solomon, 2018; Raposo et al., 2023).

Even if similar and strictly interconnected, aridity and drought refer to distinct concepts. Namely, aridity defines a condition of permanent or seasonal nature, connected with local climate characteristics, while drought originated from a temporary anomaly connected to the intrinsic weather variability, characterized by unpredictability in terms of duration and intensity (Cook et al., 2004; Diodato & Bellocchi, 2008; Lloyd, 1986; Wallén, 1967). Besides the long period climatic tendencies, Italy experienced several drought events even in traditionally less vulnerable areas, as Northern Italy, in turn worsening the condition of water deficit already reported in many central and southern regions (Perini et al., 2007; Polemio & Casarano, 2008; Rossi et al., 2023).

The relevant environmental and socioeconomic consequences of an increased level of aridity and the higher frequency of droughts constitute crucial factors triggering desertification processes (UNCCD, 2010). Within this framework, a territorial analysis should delineate the national profile of aridity regimes, with strict reference to the intensity, temporal evolution and spatial distribution of rainfalls, as well as evaluate the potential impacts on agriculture (Rahman et al., 2024; Tahat et al., 2020; Yang et al., 2024).

METHODOLOGY

Study Area

Italy extends over more than 300,000 km^2 within the Mediterranean Basin (Fig. 3.1). Its landscape is primarily characterized by hills and mountains, with plains covering a smaller portion of country's land. It represents a notable case study for aridity research, due to the remarkable differences among its three main macro-areas, i.e., North, Center, and South (Salvati & Zitti, 2009). In particular, a relevant socioeconomic gap between these macro-regions (Chelli et al., 2016, Ciommi et al., 2017, Ciommi et al., 2018) emerges along with strong differences in soil biophysical properties (Costantini et al., 2014), climate (Lanfredi et al., 2015), and vegetation cover/quality (Blasi et al., 2004). This heterogeneity allows for a detailed

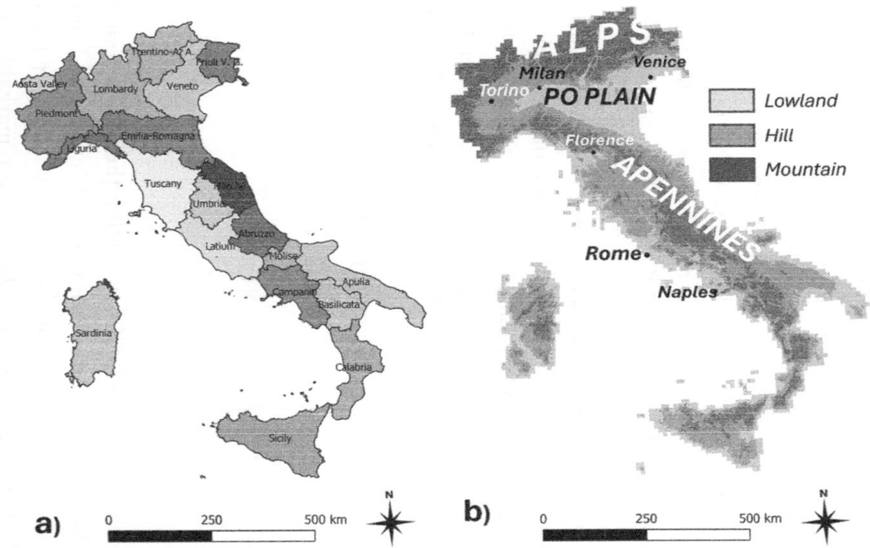

Fig. 3.1 Partitions of Italy into (a) 20 NUTS-2 Administrative Regions (Nomenclature of Territorial Units for Statistics) and (b) Elevation Categories: Lowland, Hill, and Mountain.
Source: Authors' Elaboration of Official Statistics.

examination of the intricate interactions between socio-economic and geo-environmental features shaping its territorial vulnerability to soil aridity (Salvati et al., 2008).

The gap existing between rainfall amount and water demand could be effectively quantified through the AI provided by UNEP,[1] FAO,[2] and UNCCD,[3] a rather simple tool aimed at scientific research and, at the same time, operational support for land monitoring (Arora, 2002; Greve et al., 2019; Trabucco & Zomer, 2019). The AI is represented by the ratio between the total annual precipitation (P) and annual (cumulated) evapotranspiration (ET_0) rates:

$$IA = P/ET_0$$

It represents a bioclimatic index, accounting for physical phenomena (evapotranspiration and precipitation) and biological processes (e.g., plant transpiration) as well as one of the most significant measures of early desertification processes (Beck et al., 2018; Middleton & Thomas, 1997; Nastos et al., 2013). As reported in Table 3.1, values of the index below 0.5 refer to arid or semi-arid areas; values exceeding 0.65 indicate humid or hyper-humid zones.

The meteorological data to estimate annual measures of rainfalls and evapotranspiration within the Italian territory, have been retrieved from the National Agrometeorological Database (BDAN)[4] and other official statistical sources including the National Statistical Institute (ISTAT). In particular, this work relies on daily data on Minimum Temperature (T_n), Maximum Temperature (T_x), and Precipitation (P) over the time period between 1951 and 2010 computed through the Kriging geostatistical technique at the spatial nodes of a 30 × 30 km regular grid (Libertà & Girolamo, 1991). The Kriging method interpolates the value of the variable under scrutiny, temperature or rainfall in our case, as the weighted average the observations of that variable, in all

Table 3.1 Climate Classification Based on AI Values.

AI Values	Climate Classification
$AI < 0.05$	Hyper-arid
$0.05 < AI < 0.2$	Arid
$0.2 < AI < 0.5$	Semi-arid
$0.5 < AI < 0.65$	Dry sub-humid
$0.65 < AI > 0.75$	Humid
$AI > 0.75$	Hyper-humid

points within a clearly defined spatial area (Salvati & Zitti, 2005). At first, the Hargreaves/Samani formula has been adopted to estimate the reference evapotranspiration value (ET_0). The obtained daily values of ET_0, combined with those of P, have been aggregated at the annual level, and used to compute the AI, resulting in a matrix composed of 32,640 index values (precisely 60 years × 544 grid nodes).

The spatial distribution of AI derives from a proper elaboration of the resulting data matrix through geospatial tools in a GIS (Geographic Information System) environment, after streamlining the time dimension with moving averages over a 30-year time horizon. Each grid node corresponds to an AI value computed within the periods 1951–1980; 1952–1981; 1953–1982; 1981–2010. Besides compressing the data matrix, this methodology properly filters the inter-annual variability of AI, thus providing a more reliable spatial characterization of its magnitude. The thematic maps, generated by arranging the spatial nodes in a regular grid, are the result of the Inverse Distance Weighting interpolation technique.

Data Quality Assessment

The analysis includes a statistical evaluation of data coverage, completeness, comparability, robustness, and suitability for elaboration and discussion of each thematic field to provide exhaustive environmental reporting at different geographical and temporal scales. For each field, original/new indicators and graphical/cartographical representations might be suggested and discussed considering several specific issues. These issues relate to (i) data coverage, (ii) data completeness, (iii) data comparability, (iv) data robustness, and (v) data suitability (Vardopoulos et al., 2021).

First, data coverage selects the most efficient spatial units (e.g., NUTS-0, NUTS-1, and NUTS-2 levels) allowing the comparison of the results from different geographical scales and with different spatial resolution to obtain full coverage of the whole country. A GIS tool quantifies the critical amount of coverage, e.g., by indicating critical thresholds to include/exclude specific indicators (Tomao et al., 2017). In addition, a statistical analysis of time and spatial series completeness has been performed according to the overall availability of environmental datasets provided by Eurostat and the related indicators (data completeness). GIS tools may also evaluate the effectiveness of the various indicators in providing a reliable picture of the different landscapes (Salvati & Carlucci, 2014). A specific module will, then, evaluate data comparability among selected variables and indicators by specifically addressing (a) definitions, (b) classifications, (c) data collection techniques, and (d) sampling procedures/estimation methodologies.

The resulting elementary variables and environmental indicators have been examined to prevent potential biases and inconsistencies through a validation procedure ensuring data reliability (data robustness). A general framework should be designed to evaluate the reliability and appropriateness of the available datasets based on the final data users' needs. Possible data gaps and lack of information will be highlighted along with potential strategies suitable to fill these gaps (data suitability).

EMPIRICAL RESULTS

Between 1951 and 2010, the average AI for the whole of Italy is 0.90 (Table 3.2), meaning an almost complete balance between rainfall and evapotranspiration. The measure defines a country not directly susceptible to the effects of both aridity and drought.

Throughout the analyzed period, however, fluctuating AI values highlight complex and heterogeneous dynamics connected to the different regional peculiarities along with the intrinsic climate variability associated with rainfall regimes and temperature patterns. At the national level, AI performed values ranging from 0.49 to 1.54, defining a climate gradient extending from semiarid and hyper-humid conditions along with a negative AI variation of more than 18 percentage points, over the 30-year windows 1951–1980 and 1981–2010. However, notable peculiarities emerge from the analysis of the regional level. Namely, Sicily, Sardinia, and Apulia report the lowest national AI values, corresponding to an average rainfall measure below 600 mm and an almost twice higher level of evapotranspiration.

Between 1951 and 2010, these regions registered an average AI between 0.55 and 0.60, with minimum values approaching the aridity threshold (AI < 0.2). Northern regions, characterized by more abundant rainfall compensating for the potential evapotranspiration level, performed values close to (or above) 1. Nevertheless, AI values fluctuated between a minimum of 0.5 and a maximum exceeding 3, e.g., in Aosta Valley and Friuli Venezia Giulia, as a consequence of climate variability. Regional peculiarities connected to the 30-years windows observations highlight a reduction ranging from a maximum of 28.6% in Friuli Venezia Giulia to 3.4% in Sicily (minimum value).

Table 3.2 Regional Minimum, Mean, and Maximum AI Values in Italy for 1951–2010, Alongside the Average AI and Its Percentage Change Between 1951–1980 and 1981–2010.

Region	1951–2010			1951–1980	1981–2010	% variation
	Minimum	Average	Maximum			
Abruzzo	0.45	0.78	1.22	0.84	0.71	−14.9
Basilicata	0.45	0.73	1.08	0.78	0.68	−13.1
Calabria	0.55	0.93	1.44	1.01	0.84	−17.1
Campania	0.50	0.89	1.38	1.00	0.79	−20.6
Emilia-Romagna	0.54	0.89	1.47	0.96	0.81	−15.3
Friuli-Venezia Giulia	0.89	1.56	3.01	1.82	1.30	−28.6
Lazio	0.50	0.87	1.39	0.95	0.80	−15.6
Liguria	0.48	1.07	1.81	1.19	0.95	−20.5
Lombardy	0.56	1.16	2.21	1.32	1.00	−24.2
Marche	0.52	0.90	1.40	0.99	0.81	−17.9
Molise	0.48	0.79	1.25	0.89	0.69	−22.3
Piemonte	0.54	1.15	2.12	1.28	1.01	−21.3
Apulia	0.34	0.60	0.98	0.64	0.56	−13.6
Sardinia	0.29	0.55	0.96	0.62	0.48	−22.3
Sicily	0.27	0.56	0.97	0.57	0.55	−3.4
Toscana	0.52	0.94	1.62	1.06	0.82	−22.0
Trentino-Alto Adige	0.73	1.32	2.39	1.43	1.20	−16.5
Umbria	0.53	0.92	1.45	0.99	0.84	−15.2
Aosta Valley	0.52	1.43	3.08	1.51	1.34	−11.3
Veneto	0.65	1.08	1.73	1.18	0.98	−17.2
Italy	**0.49**	**0.90**	**1.54**	**0.99**	**0.81**	**−18.4**

This evidence relates to the observed reduction in rainfall combined with an increase in temperature, causing evapotranspiration, recently worsening the conditions of aridity and persistent drought. The temporal trend of AI can easily be estimated through a time series analysis by geographical macro-area (namely, North, Center, South, and Islands). The chart highlights a pronounced geographical gradient in the temporal variability of the phenomena, with Northern regions showing much stronger fluctuations than Southern ones. The progressive aridification of Italy is exemplified by the contrasting cases of Sardinia and Friuli Venezia Giulia. During the second 30-year time span (1981–2010), Sardinia, with relatively favorable initial conditions (AI = 0.62; P = 870 mm) between 1951 and 1980, recorded an AI variation of −22.3%, below the threshold for arid areas (AI = 0.48).

It is worth noting that rainfall has decreased by 42% in Sardinia (from 506 mm). In Friuli Venezia Giulia, the magnitude of AI reduction amounted to 28.6% (from 1.82 to 1.30), triggering a decrease in rainfall of 26.0% (from 1.456 mm to 1.080 mm). Although the values of AI and rainfall contributions showed, in this latter case, an even sharper decrease, similar to the values observed for Sardinia, around 370 mm per year, the region, anyway, experienced favorable climate conditions, compared with the other areas.

Over the national territory, most AI values resulted to be higher than 0.65, which corresponds, according to the empirical classification of the AI, to "humid" or "hyper-humid" climate conditions. The deterioration in average climate conditions, observed between 1981 and 2010, once again led to a relevant drying-up process, particularly impacting Southern and Insular regions.

DISCUSSION

A careful quantitative analysis of our database illustrates the various levels of water stress connected to scarce and/or irregularly distributed rainfall over the course of the year. These conditions generate multiple impacts on both the environment and populations, which can be structurally – driven by climate (aridity) – or occasionally associated with climate variability and droughts (Ferrara et al., 2016). In this framework, recent data presented in this study highlight how Italy has experienced varying degrees of water stress, primarily due to insufficient and poorly distributed rainfall combined with sudden rises in temperature. The AI is a widely adopted and effective tool to classify the Italian territory according to the degrees of aridity and drought over a considerable period (1951–2010).

Beyond the absolute values and associated climate classifications, AI has enabled the evaluation of geographical features and regional differences, as well as their temporal variations. Over the past three decades, the most pronounced deterioration has been confined to certain parts of Italy, such as Sardinia and Sicily, while other Southern regions have remained largely unaffected. The work shows that a seasonal disaggregation of AI values would allow a more detailed description of the local environment. During autumn and winter seasons, soil succeeds in recharging effectively water reserves, since in these seasons, rainfall exceeds the evapotranspiration demand by four times (e.g. Ferrara et al., 2020).

In addition, the increased water demand typical of the spring season leads to a balance between rainfall and evapotranspiration, even if, in several Southern regions, e.g., Apulia, Sardinia, and Sicily, relevant criticalities still persist, as reported by their AI values. In summer, the almost total absence of rainfalls, combined with high temperatures and an intense solar exposure, generated conditions of marked aridity and sometimes extreme drought. In areas as Sardinia and Sicily, such conditions could even reach the typical levels of hyper-aridity (Fig. 3.2). Throughout this period, indeed, 14 out of the 20 Italian regions registered an AI below 0.5. Within this framework, the agro-systems develop an adaptive response to environmental conditions, particularly climate, and any modification able to alter ecological and bio-cenotic balances requires dedicated interventions, in coherence with environmentally sustainable land management and responsible farming methods (Mancino et al., 2016).

Fig. 3.2 Semi-arid Landscape Because of Natural Degradation Processes Under Mediterranean Ecological Conditions.
Source: Authors' Photographic Archive.

Planning and Policy Implications

Despite the articulate design and proper realization of several works of hydraulic engineering, hydro-geologic instability phenomena, although occasional, still persist, especially during particularly intense rainfalls, compromising the stability of the territorial infrastructures (Coluzzi et al., 2025). The vulnerability of national territory is connected with its complex orography and geographical position, making Italy naturally exposed to processes of continuous landscape transformation (Salvati & Carlucci, 2011). This intrinsic fragility is complemented by the pressures derived from human activities, an increasing climate variability and significant land-use changes, further accentuating the ecological risk. In many Southern areas, the persistence of aridity conditions intensifies soil erosion processes. Mixing long periods of drought and very intense rainfalls, indeed, accelerated soil deterioration (Salvati & Zitti, 2005; Salvati et al., 2008; Samela et al., 2022a).

Climate regimes show an always more evident variability, characterized by the extension of drought periods, higher frequency of extreme events, rainfalls concentration in always shorter temporal intervals and the increase in cyclic droughts (De Wrachien & Ragab, 2003). As a result, several environmental phenomena are increasing in a significant size both in extension and intensity: among them, the widening of the areas prone to drought and desertification, the increase in floods' risk, the worsening of erosion processes and landslides, and the progressive salinization of coastal areas (Carlucci et al., 2022; Imbrenda et al., 2018; Samela et al., 2022b; Scarascia et al., 2007). Water resources seem to be always more complex to manage due to the increase in their demand in all productive sectors and the always more compelling irrigation requirements (Scarascia et al., 2006).

Meanwhile, agriculture should face a set of structural criticalities, including the decrease in value added, the progressive reduction in agricultural surfaces, also due to the expansion of urbanized and sealed areas (Imbrenda et al., 2023; Pace et al., 2023; Ragosta et al., 2024), employment decreases, the aging of sectoral operators, and the increasing abandonment of productive and fertile soils (Quaranta et al., 2020). Within this framework, the effective management of ecological risks would require the introduction of a proper system of prevention, integrated by measures of territorial planning able to reduce the occurrence of chaotic events or, at least, to contain the damages (Fig. 3.2). To prevent means identifying the causes of degradation and intervene before they acquire critical dimensions (Ugolini & Mordini, 2002). For this reason, the safeguard of soil and the integrated management of water resources should be considered absolute priorities for a modern country, not only as tools of environmental protection (Fig. 3.3), but also as central elements to ensure a durable and sustainable socioeconomic development (Jakubínský et al., 2021).

Fig. 3.3 Environmental Monitoring of Weather and Landscape Conditions Based on Local Measure Stations.
Source: Authors' Photographic Archive.

CONCLUDING REMARKS

The significant interplay between climate and societal factors – such as migration, demographic pressures, and economic activities including agriculture, tourism, water pollution, and industrial hazards – highlights the need for a detailed spatial characterization of the territory. This territorial framework should be depicted by combining climatic data on both geophysical and socioeconomic components from different sources through GIS procedures, implying a significant increase in the density of measurement stations. Further steps include the implementation of indicators on the flow of water courses, such as average discharges and water volumes flowing into the sea, at the hydrographic basin level. A climatic, bioclimatic and agro-climatic analysis of the Italian territory, has been carried here as being aimed at creating a national information system. The database adopted in this contribution provides a detailed territorial coverage and includes the main primary and derived quantities of interest, as those used to determine the vulnerability of the territory. Furthermore, analyzing historical data allows for the identification of trends in precipitation and temperature in light of territorial characteristics, highlighting stress situations for the agro-ecosystem.

NOTES

1. United Nations Environment Programme (http://www.unep.org/).

2. Food and Agriculture Organization (http://www.fao.org/).

3. United Nations Convention to Combat Desertification (http://www.unccd.int/main.php).

4. The National Agrometeorological Database (BDAN) is a centralized digital repository developed as part of the National Agricultural Information System (SIAN) of the Ministry of Agriculture, Food Sovereignty and Forestry (MASAF). It collects primary observational records acquired from meteorological stations operated by multiple national and local monitoring networks, including the Air Force, the former Hydrographic and Mareographic Service, as well as several regional agro-meteorological services. Beyond raw observational measurements, BDAN also provides a wide range of derived climate statistics and specialized agrometeorological datasets (https://www.crea.gov.it/en/web/agricoltura-e-ambiente/-/national-meteorological-archive).

REFERENCES

Allen, R. G. (2000). *Crop evapotranspiration: Guidelines for computing crop water requirements* (repr). Food and Agriculture Organization of the United Nations.

Arora, V. K. (2002). The use of the aridity index to assess climate change effect on annual runoff. *Journal of Hydrology, 265*(1–4), 164–177. https://doi.org/10.1016/s0022-1694(02)00101-4

Beck, H. E., Zimmermann, N. E., McVicar, T. R., Vergopolan, N., Berg, A., & Wood, E. F. (2018). Present and future Köppen-Geiger climate classification maps at 1-km resolution. *Scientific Data, 5*(1), 1–12.

Berdugo, M., Delgado-Baquerizo, M., Soliveres, S., Hernández-Clemente, R., Zhao, Y., Gaitán, J. J., Gross, N., Saiz, H., Maire, V., Lehmann, A., Rillig, M. C., Solé, R. V., & Maestre, F. T. (2020). Global ecosystem thresholds driven by aridity. *Science, 367*(6479), 787–790. https://doi.org/10.1126/science.aay5958

Biasi, R., Brunori, E., Ferrara, C., & Salvati, L. (2019). Assessing impacts of climate change on phenology and quality traits of Vitis vinifera L.: The contribution of local knowledge. *Plants, 8*(5), 121.

Blasi, C., Filibeck, G., Frondoni, R., Rosati, L., & Smiraglia, D. (2004). The map of the vegetation series of Italy. *Fitosociologia, 41*, 21–25.

Brunetti, M., Maugeri, M., Monti, F., & Nanni, T. (2006a). Temperature and precipitation variability in Italy in the last two centuries from homogenised instrumental time series. *International Journal of Climatology*, 26(3), 345–381. https://doi.org/10.1002/joc.1251

Brunetti, M., Maugeri, M., Monti, F., & Nanni, T. (2006b). The variability and change of Italian climate in the last 160 years. *Il Nuovo Cimento C, 29*(1), 3–12. https://doi.org/10.1393/ncc/i2005-10215-1

Brunetti, M., Maugeri, M., Nanni, T., Auer, I., Böhm, R., & Schöner, W. (2006c). Precipitation variability and changes in the greater Alpine region over the 1800–2003 period. Journal of Geophysical Research: Atmospheres, 111(D11).

Carlucci, M., Salvia, R., Quaranta, G., Salvati, L., & Imbrenda, V. (2022). Official statistics, spatio-temporal dynamics and local-scale monitoring: Toward integrated environmental-economic accounting for land degradation. *Letters in Spatial and Resource Sciences, 15*(3), 469–491.

Chelli, F. M., Ciommi, M., Emili, A., Gigliarano, C., & Taralli, S. (2016). Assessing the equitable and sustainable well-being of the Italian provinces. *International Journal of Uncertainty, Fuzziness and Knowledge-Based Systems*, *24*(Suppl. 1), 39–62.

Ciommi, M., Chelli, F. M., Carlucci, M., & Salvati, L. (2018). Urban growth and demographic dynamics in Southern Europe: Toward a new statistical approach to regional science. *Sustainability*, *10*, 2765.

Ciommi, M., Gentili, A., Ermini, B., Gigliarano, C., Chelli, F. M., & Gallegati, M. (2017). Have your cake and eat it too: The well-being of the Italians (1861–2011). *Social Indicators Research*, *134*(2), 473–509.

Colantoni, A., Ferrara, C., Perini, L., & Salvati, L. (2015). Assessing trends in climate aridity and vulnerability to soil degradation in Italy. *Ecological Indicators*, *48*, 599–604. https://doi.org/10.1016/j.ecolind.2014.09.031

Coluzzi, R., Perrone, A., Samela, C., Imbrenda, V., Manfreda, S., Pace, L., & Lanfredi, M. (2025). Rapid landslide detection from free optical satellite imagery using a robust change detection technique. *Scientific Reports*, *15*(1), 4697.

Cook, E. R., Woodhouse, C. A., Eakin, C. M., Meko, D. M., & Stahle, D. W. (2004). Long-Term Aridity Changes in the Western United States. *Science*, *306*(5698), 1015–1018. https://doi.org/10.1126/science.1102586

Costantini, E. A. C., Barbetti, R., Fantappiè, M., L'Abate, G., Lorenzetti, R., Napoli, R., & Rivieccio, R. (2014). *The soil map of Italy: A hierarchy of geodatabases, from soil regions to sub-systems* (pp. 109–112). Global Soil Map; Taylor & Francis.

De Wrachien, D., & Ragab, R. (2003). *Variabilità climatica e suo impatto sul bilancio disponibilità idriche e fabbisogni irrigui nel bacino del Mediterraneo* (pp. 77–97). Atti del Congresso Internazionale ANBI-FAO.

Diodato, N., & Bellocchi, G. (2008). Drought stress patterns in Italy using agro-climatic indicators. *Climate Research*, *36*, 53–63. https://doi.org/10.3354/cr00726

Dore, M. H. I. (2005). Climate change and changes in global precipitation patterns: What do we know? *Environment International*, *31*(8), 1167–1181. https://doi.org/10.1016/j.envint.2005.03.004

Ferrara, A., Kelly, C., Wilson, G. A., Nolè, A., Mancino, G., Bajocco, S., & Salvati, L. (2016). Shaping the role of 'fast' and 'slow' drivers of change in forest-shrubland socio-ecological systems. *Journal of Environmental Management*, *169*, 155–166.

Ferrara, A., Kosmas, C., Salvati, L., Padula, A., Mancino, G., & Nolè, A. (2020). Updating the MEDALUS-ESA framework for worldwide land degradation and desertification assessment. *Land Degradation & Development*, *31*(12), 1593–1607.

Francaviglia, R., Di Bene, C., Farina, R., Salvati, L., & Vicente-Vicente, J. L. (2019). Assessing "4 per 1000" soil organic carbon storage rates under Mediterranean climate: A comprehensive data analysis. *Mitigation and Adaptation Strategies for Global Change*, *24*, 795–818.

Fratianni, S., & Acquaotta, F. (2017). The Climate of Italy. In M. Soldati & M. Marchetti (A c. Di), *Landscapes and landforms of Italy* (pp. 29–38). Springer International Publishing. https://doi.org/10.1007/978-3-319-26194-2_4

Greve, P., Roderick, M. L., Ukkola, A. M., & Wada, Y. (2019). The aridity Index under global warming. *Environmental Research Letters*, *14*(12), 124006. https://doi.org/10.1088/1748-9326/ab5046

Huang, J., Du, D., & Tao, Q. (2017). An analysis of technological factors and energy intensity in China. *Energy Policy*, 109, 1–9.

Imbrenda, V., Coluzzi, R., Lanfredi, M., Loperte, A., Satriani, A., & Simoniello, T. (2018). Analysis of landscape evolution in a vulnerable coastal area under natural and human pressure. *Geomatics, Natural Hazards and Risk*, 9(1), 1249–1279.

Imbrenda, V., Gómez, C. M., D'Emilio, M., Samela, C., Salvati, L., Matarazzo, N., Lanfredi, M., & Coluzzi, R. (2023). Remote sensing and spatial databases for investigating latent urban-rural dynamics in rural, inland districts of Southern Italy. *Cuadernos de investigación geográfica: Geographical Research Letters*, 49(2), 143–162.

Incerti, G., Feoli, E., Salvati, L., Brunetti, A., & Giovacchini, A. (2007). Analysis of bioclimatic time series and their neural network-based classification to characterise drought risk patterns in South Italy. *International Journal of Biometeorology*, *51*, 253–263.

Jakubínský, J., Prokopová, M., Raška, P., Salvati, L., Bezak, N., Cudlín, O., Cudlín, P., Purkyt, J., Vezza, P., Camporeale, C., Daněk, J., Pástor, M., & Lepeška, T. (2021). Managing floodplains using nature-based solutions to support multiple ecosystem functions and services. *Wiley Interdisciplinary Reviews: Water*, *8*(5), e1545.

Kosmas, C., Detsis, V., Karamesouti, M., Kounalaki, K., Vassiliou, P., & Salvati, L. (2015). Exploring long-term impact of grazing management on land degradation in the socio-ecological system of Asteroussia Mountains, Greece. *Land*, *4*(3), 541–559.

Lanfredi, M., Coluzzi, R., Imbrenda, V., Macchiato, M., & Simoniello, T. (2020). Analyzing space–time coherence in precipitation seasonality across different European climates. *Remote Sensing*, *12*(1), 171.

Lanfredi, M., Coppola, R., D'Emilio, M., Imbrenda, V., Macchiato, M., & Simoniello, T. (2015). A geostatistics-assisted approach to the deterministic approximation of climate data. *Environmental Modelling & Software*, *66*, 69–77.

Libertà, A., & Girolamo, A. (1991). Geostatistical analysis of the average temperature fields in North Italy in the period 1961 to 1985. *Sciences de la terre. Informatique géologique*, (30), 1–36.

Lickley, M., & Solomon, S. (2018). Drivers, timing and some impacts of global aridity change. *Environmental Research Letters*, *13*(10), 104010. https://doi.org/10.1088/1748-9326/aae013

Lloyd, J. W. (1986). A review of aridity and groundwater. *Hydrological Processes*, *1*(1), 63–78. https://doi.org/10.1002/hyp.3360010107

Luppichini, M., Bini, M., Barsanti, M., Giannecchini, R., & Zanchetta, G. (2022). Seasonal rainfall trends of a key Mediterranean area in relation to large-scale atmospheric circulation: How does current global change affect the rainfall regime? *Journal of Hydrology*, *612*, 128233. https://doi.org/10.1016/j.jhydrol.2022.128233

Mancino, G., Nolè, A., Salvati, L., & Ferrara, A. (2016). In-between forest expansion and cropland decline: A revised USLE model for soil erosion risk under land-use change in a Mediterranean region. *Ecological Indicators*, *71*, 544–550.

Messeri, A., Morabito, M., Messeri, G., Brandani, G., Petralli, M., Natali, F., Grifoni, D., Crisci, A., Gensini, G., & Orlandini, S. (2015). Weather-related flood and landslide damage: A risk index for Italian regions. *PLOS ONE*, *10*(12), e0144468. https://doi.org/10.1371/journal.pone.0144468

Middleton, N., & Thomas, D. S. G. (1997). *World atlas of desertification* (2nd ed.). Arnold; Copublished in the US, Central and South America by John Wiley.

Molinié, G., Ceresetti, D., Anquetin, S., Creutin, J. D., & Boudevillain, B. (2012). Rainfall regime of a mountainous Mediterranean Region: Statistical analysis at short time steps. *Journal of Applied Meteorology and Climatology*, *51*(3), 429–448. https://doi.org/10.1175/2011jamc2691.1

Nastos, P. T., Politi, N., & Kapsomenakis, J. (2013). Spatial and temporal variability of the Aridity Index in Greece. *Atmospheric Research*, *119*, 140–152. https://doi.org/10.1016/j.atmosres.2011.06.017

Pace, L., Imbrenda, V., Lanfredi, M., Cudlín, P., Simoniello, T., Salvati, L., & Coluzzi, R. (2023). Delineating the intrinsic, long-term path of land degradation: A spatially explicit transition matrix for Italy, 1960–2010. *International Journal of Environmental Research and Public Health*, *20*(3), 2402. https://doi.org/10.3390/ijerph20032402

Perini, L., Salvati, L., Ceccarelli, T., Caruso, T., Motisi, A., & Marra, F. P. (2007). *Atlante agroclimatico. Scenari di cambiamento climatico (Con DVD)* (p. 82). CRA-CMA. ISBN: 978-88-9014-728-9.

Polemio, M., & Casarano, D. (2008). Climate change, drought and groundwater availability in southern Italy. *Geological Society, London, Special Publications*, *288*(1), 39–51. https://doi.org/10.1144/sp288.4

Quaranta, G., Salvia, R., Salvati, L., Paola, V. D., Coluzzi, R., Imbrenda, V., & Simoniello, T. (2020). Long-term impacts of grazing management on land degradation in a rural community of Southern Italy: Depopulation matters. *Land Degradation & Development*, *31*(16), 2379–2394. https://doi.org/10.1002/ldr.3583

Ragosta, M., Daniele, G., Imbrenda, V., Coluzzi, R., D'Emilio, M., Lanfredi, M., & Matarazzo, N. (2024). Land transformations in Irpinia (Southern Italy): A tale on the socio-economic dynamics acting in a marginal area of the Mediterranean Europe. *Sustainability*, *16*(19), 8724. https://doi.org/10.3390/su16198724

Rahman, Md. M., Biswas, J. C., & Meena, R. S. (A c. Di). (2024). *Climate change and soil-water-plant nexus: Agriculture and environment*. Springer Nature Singapore. https://doi.org/10.1007/978-981-97-6635-2

Raposo, V. D. M. B., Costa, V. A. F., & Rodrigues, A. F. (2023). A review of recent developments on drought characterization, propagation, and influential factors. *Science of The Total Environment*, *898*, 165550. https://doi.org/10.1016/j.scitotenv.2023.165550

Rossi, L., Naumann, G., Gabellani, S., & Cammalleri, C. (2023). A combined index to characterize agricultural drought in Italy at municipality scale. *Journal of Hydrology: Regional Studies*, *47*, 101404. https://doi.org/10.1016/j.ejrh.2023.101404

Salvati, L., & Carlucci, M. (2011). The economic and environmental performances of rural districts in Italy: Are competitiveness and sustainability compatible targets? *Ecological Economics*, *70*(12), 2446–2453.

Salvati, L., & Carlucci, M. (2014). A composite index of sustainable development at the local scale: Italy as a case study. *Ecological Indicators*, *43*, 162–171.

Salvati, L., Mavrakis, A., Colantoni, A., Mancino, G., & Ferrara, A. (2015). Complex Adaptive Systems, soil degradation and land sensitivity to desertification: A multivariate assessment of Italian agro-forest landscape. *Science of the Total Environment*, *521*, 235–245.

Salvati, L., Petitta, M., Ceccarelli, T., Perini, L., Di Battista, F., & Scarascia, M. E. V. (2008). Italy's renewable water resources as estimated on the basis of the monthly water balance. *Irrigation and Drainage: The Journal of the International Commission on Irrigation and Drainage*, *57*(5), 507–515.

Salvati, L., & Zitti, M. (2005). Land degradation in the Mediterranean basin: Linking bio-physical and economic factors into an ecological perspective. *Biota*, 6, 67–77.

Salvati, L., & Zitti, M. (2009). The environmental "risky" region: Identifying land degradation processes through integration of socio-economic and ecological indicators in a multivariate regionalization model. *Environmental Management*, *44*(5), 888–898.

Salvati, L., Zitti, M., & Ceccarelli, T. (2008). Integrating economic and environmental indicators in the assessment of desertification risk: A case study. *Applied Ecological and Environmental Research*, 6(1), 129–138.

Samela, C., Coluzzi, R., Imbrenda, V., Manfreda, S., & Lanfredi, M. (2022b). Satellite flood detection integrating hydrogeomorphic and spectral indices. *GIScience & Remote Sensing*, *59*(1), 1997–2018.

Samela, C., Imbrenda, V., Coluzzi, R., Pace, L., Simoniello, T., & Lanfredi, M. (2022a). Multi-decadal assessment of soil loss in a Mediterranean region characterized by contrasting local climates. *Land*, *11*(7), 1010.

Scarascia, M. E. V., Battista, F. D., & Salvati, L. (2006). Water resources in Italy: Availability and agricultural uses. *Irrigation and Drainage*, *55*(2), 115–127. https://doi.org/10.1002/ird.222

Scarascia, M. E. V., Perini, L., Ceccarelli, T., Ranuzzi, M., Zitti, M., & Salvati, L. (2007*). Ecosistemi sotto pressione nel Lazio*. Ed.Geva, Roma.

Tahat, M. M., Alananbeh, K. M., Othman, Y. A., & Leskovar, D. I. (2020). Soil health and sustainable agriculture. *Sustainability*, *12*(12), 4859. https://doi.org/10.3390/su12124859

Tomao, A., Quatrini, V., Corona, P., Ferrara, A., Lafortezza, R., & Salvati, L. (2017). Resilient landscapes in Mediterranean urban areas: Understanding factors influencing forest trends. *Environmental Research*, *156*, 1–9.

Trabucco, A., & Zomer, R. (2019). *Global Aridity Index and Potential Evapotranspiration (ET0) Climate Database v2*. https://doi.org/10.6084/M9.FIGSHARE.7504448.V3

Ugolini, M., & Mordini, L. (2002). I progetti di riqualificazione ambientale per la tutela del paesaggio montano. Conoscenza dell'ambiente e rischio idrogeologico. Atti Convegno Nazionale CNR, IRPI, GNDCI. *Conservazione dell'ambiente e rischio idrogeologico*, 695–706.

UNCCD. (2010). *Water scarcity and desertification. UNCCD Thematic factsheet series N. 2*. http://www.unccd.int/documents/Desertification andwater.pdf

Vardopoulos, I., Tsilika, E., Sarantakou, E., Zorpas, A. A., Salvati, L., & Tsartas, P. (2021). An integrated SWOT-PESTLE-AHP model assessing sustainability in adaptive reuse projects. *Applied Sciences*, *11*(15), 7134.

Wallén, C. C. (1967). Aridity definitions and their applicability. *Geografiska Annaler: Series A, Physical Geography*, *49*(2–4), 367–384. https://doi.org/10.1080/04353676.1967.11879765

Yang, Y., Tilman, D., Jin, Z., Smith, P., Barrett, C. B., Zhu, Y.-G., Burney, J., D'Odorico, P., Fantke, P., Fargione, J., Finlay, J. C., Rulli, M. C., Sloat, L., Jan Van Groenigen, K., West, P. C., Ziska, L., Michalak, A. M., the Clim-Ag Team, Lobell, D. B., & Zhuang, M. (2024). Climate change exacerbates the environmental impacts of agriculture. *Science*, *385*(6713), eadn3747. https://doi.org/10.1126/science.adn3747

4

GLOBAL WARMING, DROUGHT, AND SOIL PROTECTION IN RURAL LANDSCAPES

GIUSEPPE CILLIS[a], NADIA MATARAZZO[b], MARIAGRAZIA D'EMILIO[a], MARCO MAIALETTI[c], DONATO SCARPITTA[d], ADELE SATERIANO[e], IOANNIS KONAXIS[f] AND ALESSIA D'AGATA[g]

[a]National Research Council of Italy, Institute of Methodologies for Environmental Analysis (CNR-IMAA), Italy
[b]'Federico II' University of Naples, Italy
[c]Independent Researcher and Lawyer, Italy
[d]Independent Researcher and Architect, Italy
[e]Mediterranean Sustainable Development Foundation (MEDES), Italy
[f]University of Piraeus, Greece
[g]Sapienza University of Rome, Italy

ABSTRACT

The present chapter addresses climate aridity and drought in natural and agricultural environments within Mediterranean Italy, proposing a quantitative analysis based on diversified tools and methodologies. The first part of this work deals with territorial planning at the river-basin scale, aimed at containing the effects of drought and aridity, and their socioeconomic impacts. Within this context, preventive actions have been identified to respond to the ongoing changes in climate regimes. Moreover, the study focuses on the implementation of a geo-spatial Decision Support System designed for the permanent monitoring of drought conditions and land vulnerability over the national territory. The system relies on three crucial components: (i) a meteorological module for processing high-resolution climatic variables over the whole country; (ii) a composite indicator evaluating drought intensity; and (iii) a summary index of land vulnerability integrating climatic, soil, and land-use information, allowing an expedited estimation of the ecological risk in sensitive areas. The adopted framework highlights the need for an integrated approach to spatial planning, coordinating interdisciplinary expertise and the involvement of multiple stakeholders.

Keywords: Drought; vulnerability; agriculture; land degradation; Italy

INTRODUCTION

In recent years, climatic conditions have been characterized by intrinsic, but relevant, variability, with increasingly longer periods of drought and more frequent extreme events (Canfora et al., 2017; De Wrachien & Ragab, 2003; Francaviglia et al., 2019). The observed short periods of rainfall, in turn, imply a persistent (cyclical) aridity (Lanfredi et al., 2020; Salvati et al., 2008, Biasi et al., 2019). These recent climatic dynamics increase the number of places vulnerable to soil aridity and early desertification, being instead more subject to flooding, erosion, and landslides, as well as intense (or increasing) salinization processes in coastal areas (Imbrenda et al., 2013; Pace et al., 2023; Scarascia et al., 2006). The contextual water crisis raises demand across all sectors, particularly for crop irrigation (Scarascia et al., 2006) and tourism facilities (Cillis et al., 2025). Among others, challenges in the agricultural sector arise from the ongoing decline in both added value and the extent of Utilized Agricultural Areas (UAA), primarily connected to an increase in urban and impermeable areas (Egidi et al., 2020; Imbrenda et al., 2023, Ragosta et al., 2024). A contextual decline in agricultural employment then emerged, because of farmers' ageing, and a gradual abandonment of land (Cicco et al., 2025; ISTAT, 2003; Quaranta et al., 2020; Sallustio et al., 2018).

Despite substantial public investment and comprehensive legislation, the assessment of natural disasters still requires a "paradigm shift" in optimal land management (e.g., Wilson et al., 2017). Within this framework, river basins represent an optimal governance unit for environmental analysis and efficient planning (Tomao et al., 2017). Effective legislation is required to establish a comprehensive "disaster prevention system," incorporating land redevelopment measures to mitigate the occurrence of disasters (Mancino et al., 2016). This "disaster prevention system" should detect and analyze the causes of degradation processes aimed at preventing or, at least, containing their negative effects (Ugolini & Mordini, 2002). Soil protection and water regulation measures should be promoted to design a modern state, in coherence with environmental purposes to pursue the country's sustainable socio-economic development (Kairis et al., 2014; Salvati, 2013; Seifollahi-Aghmiuni et al., 2022).

This chapter analyzes climatic aridity and drought dynamics in rural and natural environments based on several tools and strategies within the Mediterranean context. In particular, the first part of the chapter focuses on river basin-scale interventions for mitigation and damage reduction in light of sustainable development (e.g., Salvati & Carlucci, 2014). The last part of the chapter presents an operational approach to monitor land vulnerability and frequency of drought episodes, and to support adaptive planning in regions where water scarcity and land degradation increasingly threaten both productivity and resilience of ecosystems (Salvati & Zitti, 2005).

Understanding Climate Aridity with Landscape Analysis

The term "drought" usually defines a "significant, temporary reduction in water availability below the expected amount for a specified period and for a defined climatic zone" (Salvati, Scarascia, et al., 2009). In the recent literature, three different typologies have been classified according to their determinants and impacts on the socio-ecological system, i.e., meteorological, hydrological, and agricultural drought (Fig. 4.1). Namely, meteorological drought usually refers to an assessment of rainfall deficit, while hydrological drought also evaluates the balance between water inflows and outflows (Salvati & Zitti, 2009).

Lastly, agricultural drought separately evaluates its duration and intensity through the assessment of the levels of the integrated index of drought severity (Scarascia et al., 2006). To this purpose, drought duration refers to how long dry spells persist, while drought intensity measures the magnitude of the resulting water deficit, calculated using a simplified water balance that considers both precipitation and reference evapotranspiration (Ligetvari & Szalai, 2004). The observed increasing frequency of such events requires a "disaster prevention system," including measures to prevent or at least contain such episodes (e.g., Salvati et al., 2012).

Fig. 4.1 Mediterranean Agro-Forest Landscapes Adapted to Structural Drought Conditions.
Source: Authors' Photographic Archive.

A RIVER-BASIN ANALYSIS OF DROUGHT EPISODES

Hydrogeological instability usually originates from the formation of inflows in the hydrographic network and the sediment transport processes within the basin, consequently impacting downstream areas (Armanini, 1999). The catchment area is the geographical unit of reference for analyzing the hydrological cycle. Its final performance is governed by its reaction to precipitation stress and is influenced by multiple factors. The basin's geo-morphometric assessment, including its parameters and their relative importance – such as slope, lithology, drainage, and land use – allows determining its susceptibility to instability events (e.g., Incerti et al., 2007). The basin's response to rainfall, particularly regarding infiltration processes, runoff timing, and the spatial-temporal distribution of runoff, forms the basis of its functional model (Preti, 2002).

The establishment of the catchment area, functioning as an administrative-territorial entity, enables the identification and mitigation of instability factors to promote the sustainable and coordinated management of land resources, such as water, soil, and forests (Leone, 2004). In the early planning phase, prevention is implemented by analyzing and evaluating the key parameters of the catchment area. The speed and volume of the water film forming on the soil after rainfall are affected by various factors (e.g., rainfall regime and water erosion, infiltration capacity of the different soil horizons, morphology of the river basin, runoff coefficient, soil moisture, peak water-holding capacity).

In this perspective, the runoff coefficient is influenced by multiple factors, including the steepness of the terrain, the geological and pedological characteristics of the soil and its susceptibility to erosion, as well as land-use patterns and vegetation cover (Salvati & Zitti, 2008). The computation of river basin hydrological balance provides useful information on the runoff coefficient, the flow rate at the basin closure section, and the correlation coefficient.

Land Planning

The follow-up phase of prevention efforts identifies the factors leading to territorial instability. A special focus deserves the relationship between precipitation, i.e., the main triggering factor, and the most vulnerable areas of the basin. A reduction in soil vulnerability requires interventions capable of modifying the way in which the different components of the basin respond to rainfall events (e.g., Colantoni et al., 2015). In the initial stages, rainwater moves across the soil surface, partially saturating it while also infiltrating into deeper layers. However, part of the water flows as surface runoff, promoting the detachment of the upper soil stratum and the transport of soil particles (Salvati et al., 2011).

As the process develops, small water streams tend to concentrate along slopes, progressively increasing their discharge. This aspect intensifies erosion processes and may trigger landslides, leading to the formation of increasingly deeper channels and larger volumes of flowing water (Ferrara et al., 2017). The evolution of these mechanisms is sharply affected by the intensity and erosive energy of rainfall, which can be assessed by inspecting meteorological and climatic data collected by local monitoring stations (Perini, 2004). At the same time, the physical characteristics of the basin, such as basin shape and slope, soil texture, structure and depth, water retention capacity, infiltration rates, runoff dynamics, and discharge at the basin outlet, all contribute to determining the system's vulnerability and its overall response to precipitation events (Kosmas et al., 2015). The vulnerability of a basin largely depends on how the land is used (Ferrara et al., 2016). Impermeable areas, such as urban settlements, buildings, commercial zones, roads, and industrial sites, reduce the soil's ability to absorb rainfall (e.g., Ferrara et al., 2020).

As a result, precipitation tends to flow rapidly over the surface, leading to increased runoff and, as these surfaces expand, to higher flow rates. On the other hand, vegetated soils play a key role in mitigating the effects of rainfall

(Kairis et al., 2014). Vegetation reduces the direct impact of raindrops, promotes water infiltration into the soil, and increases its capacity to retain moisture, thanks to the presence of roots that make the soil more porous. A significant portion of rainfall is also returned to the atmosphere through evapotranspiration processes (Scarascia et al., 2006). Nevertheless, the effectiveness of this protective function varies largely depending on the vegetation type. In this context, the parameter known as the "curve number" is a valuable tool for assessing the protective capacity of different land covers (Kosmas et al., 2015).

According to the classification developed by the United States Soil Conservation Service, forested areas provide the highest level of protection, particularly in hilly and mountainous regions. These are followed by grasslands and permanent meadows, then tree crops, and finally, annual crops. To provide effective forest protection, proper management is essential. Practices such as removing dead or diseased trees, pruning, thinning, and restoring areas affected by wildfires help maintain healthy forest conditions. The existence of understory vegetation strengthens the system's protective function, while surface litter is essential for dissipating the kinetic energy of raindrops and maintaining soil integrity (Fig. 4.2).

Fig. 4.2 Herbaceous Crops Integrated with Traditional Tree Crops in Mediterranean Rural Landscapes.
Source: Authors' Photographic Archive.

Grasslands and pastures, although characterized by less intensive land use, also require careful and continuous management. Without appropriate practices, they may lose their beneficial role and negatively affect ecosystem balance. Finally, tree crops can make a significant contribution to regulating water runoff, especially when properly established. Planting following the natural contours of the terrain, adopting suitable drainage systems, and selecting appropriate species, allows for high levels of soil protection (Sallustio et al., 2018).

Intervention Strategies

A further stage of the prevention process aims at designing peculiar interventions for each basin based on the factors affecting the transition from inflows to outflows (Passino, 2002). To this purpose, a river basin plan should be prepared, defining all interventions required to modify the structural features of the basin. This plan develops proper structural measures along with preventive actions based on innovative and low-impact techniques (Biasi et al., 2019; Incerti et al., 2007; Salvati et al., 2008).

A preliminary measure, aimed at reshaping the first hydrographic network, includes several interventions enabling the basin to collect and efficiently evacuate stormwater, such as reducing the slope by removing tree canopy and creating terraces and embankments to modify the topography of steep terrain (Mancino et al., 2016). These interventions, aimed at promoting the percolation of larger amounts of rainwater into the soil, and consolidating land at risk of landslides, should be implemented in areas equipped with both surface and subsurface drainage infrastructure. The process ends with the plantation of suitable vegetation species (Puglisi, 2002).

The progressive abandonment of land, temporarily unproductive and subsequently colonized by spontaneous vegetation (grass cover, shrubs, and trees), since no longer managed by farmers, significantly contributes to a lack of maintenance of the territory, in turn, fueling hydrogeological instability (Coluzzi et al., 2025). According to the empirical literature dealing with agroforestry ecosystems, efficient management practices should be designed to effectively safeguard the territory and partially contain hydrogeological instability (Baldi et al., 1994). However, even protected areas require proper and rational management, carried out by highly specialized personnel, also in charge of avoiding overgrazing, with the final objective of reducing soil instability and loss of biodiversity (Quaranta et al., 2020).

GEO-SPATIAL DECISION SUPPORT SYSTEMS

The collection and dissemination of meteorological data carried out by the Italian National Institute of Statistics (ISTAT) has recently been improved. The aim of this activity includes the massive development of a comprehensive geographical data warehouse compiling daily meteorological, agro-meteorological, and hydrological measurements from a large set of gauging stations (Fig. 4.3). These data, dating back to 1951, are supplied by institutions operating at national, regional, and local levels (Colantoni et al., 2015; Ferrara et al., 2017; Salvati et al., 2011).

The activity seeks to map Italian institutions managing gauging networks and integrate their data into a geographic warehouse to support efficient environmental monitoring. Meteorological networks operate through national and regional agencies, including rural development bodies, and local research institutions. The data warehouse should enable the estimation of high spatial resolution climate variables. Indicators describing climate interactions with biological, agronomic, pedological, and hydrological variables can be derived via downscaling across administrative units – such as municipalities, local

Fig. 4.3 A Traditional Gauging Station Monitoring Instantaneous Weather Conditions in Mediterranean Landscapes.
Source: Authors' Photographic Archive.

labor systems, and homogeneous agricultural regions – to complement associated socioeconomic data.

This section describes a GIS-based monitoring scheme evaluating drought severity at a detailed geographical and temporal scale. The framework develops in three phases, starting from (i) a statistical survey to create a wide dataset summarizing meteorological phenomena. In addition, (ii) an empirical analysis implements a composite index of drought severity, based on drought duration and intensity. Finally, (iii) a drought vulnerability index for land is derived from the integrated analysis of multiple data sources and preliminary indicators. The last section discusses the implications of permanent drought assessment policies for mitigating drought risk in the Mediterranean basin.

The official survey included more than 600 institutions, among which national meteorological services, regional authorities, and local agencies dealing with environmental issues. Respondents have been chosen according to targeted web searches, complemented with additional information based on data from major national meteorological services and consultations with regional and local experts. The empirical data originate from a 2008 statistical survey conducted using software tools. Metadata for each station was gathered via computer-assisted telephone interviews (CATI) with the respective network manager. A geo-database, developed in ORACLE/ARCGIS platforms, properly stores time series data on the analyzed climatic parameters. A specialized module generates environmental climate indicators across sectors such as agriculture, public health, tourism, and water resources, providing outputs at daily, weekly, monthly, and annual intervals. The newly developed geo-statistical module provides climate data for the whole national territory at the appropriate spatial scale.

A Drought Index for Italy

Among other methods for computing the incidence of drought, the chosen method also provides a quantitative assessment of drought episodes. An elementary drought index, computed based on 2 input variables, namely rainfall and evapotranspiration, synthesizes the different aspects of drought severity, identifying conditions that can be considered "normal," from both statistical and ecological viewpoints. In this context, a Drought Severity Index (DSI) was computed according to the methodology reported in Salvati et al. (2008). DSI allows agricultural drought to be monitored, particularly when data availability is limited to temperature and precipitation. Only meteorological stations with at least 97% valid daily precipitation observations and 95% valid daily maximum and minimum temperature observations over the investigated time window were retained.

Daily reference evapotranspiration (ET_0, expressed as mm day^{-1}) was determined according to the Hargreaves–Samani formula, based on daily minimum and maximum temperature measures. Water deficit was then calculated as the average value between precipitation and potential evapotranspiration over selected time periods. Fig. 4.4 exemplifies the spatial distribution of the DSI across Italy during the severe drought episode that occurred in July 2003. The index is expressed as percentiles, with higher values corresponding to increasing drought severity.

The computation of the Drought Severity Index (DSI) follows a multi-step procedure. First, dry days and the corresponding time periods are identified; second, the climatology of dry periods is established; third, anomalies are quantified using climate percentiles; fourth, drought conditions are assessed through partial indicators related to duration and intensity; finally, agricultural drought severity is estimated using the DSI (Salvati et al., 2008). This index represents an effective tool for analyzing general climatic conditions in each geographical area, providing a concise characterization of drought events that

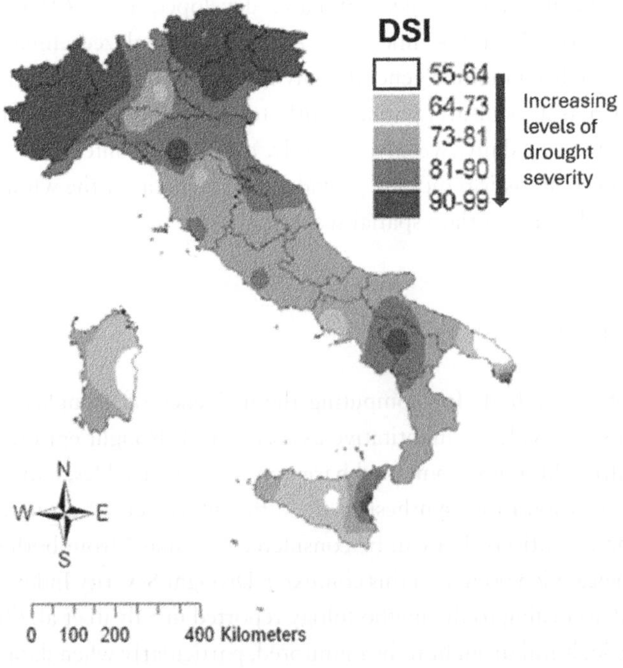

Fig. 4.4 The DSI in Italy During a Drought Episode in July 2003. DSI Is Expressed as Percentile (Higher Values Indicate Increasing Severity).
Source: Authors' Elaboration of Official Statistics.

considers both the persistence of dry periods and the overall hydrological balance. Owing to these characteristics, DSI is particularly suitable for investigating the interactions between climate change and environmental issues.

Evaluating Land Vulnerability to Drought

The third module aimed at producing maps quantifying exposure to drought based on the intensity of agricultural practices, population density, and other human activities. The module implements the Land Vulnerability Index (LVI) presented in Salvati et al. (2009). This index, including 15 thematic indicators (Table 4.1), was derived at a spatial resolution of 1 km^2. The LVI relies on

Table 4.1 LVI Dimensions, Variables Used (and Their Abbreviation), Units of Measurement, and Data Sources (S.C.: Sensitivity Classes).

Theme	Variable	Sign	Unit of Measure	Source
Soil quality	Soil depth (DEP)	–	Mm	MASAF[a]
	Organic carbon content (CAR)	–	%	MASAF
	Available water capacity (AWC)	–	Mm	MASAF
	Soil texture (TEX)	+	S.C.	MASAF
	Estimated erosion risk (ERO)	+	t ha^{-1} y^{-1}	EU Joint Research Centre
Climate	Aridity index (ARI)	+	mm mm^{-1}	Meteorological statistics
	Average annual rainfall (RAI)	–	Mn	Meteorological statistics
	Rainfall variability (RVA)	+	SD/mean (%)	Meteorological statistics
	Rainfall concentration (RCO)	+	mm mm^{-1}	Meteorological statistics
	Number of rainy days (NRD)	–	d y^{-1}	Meteorological statistics
Land use	Vegetation quality (VEG)	–	S.C.	CORINE Land Cover
	Population density (POP)	+	Inh/km^2	Household Census
	Decadal Demographic variation (DEM)	+	%	Household Census
	Agricultural intensification (INT)	+	S.C.	CORINE Land Cover

Note: [a]Italian Ministry of Agriculture, Food Sovereignty and Forests (MASAF).

a multivariate approach quantifying the contribution of each environmental indicator to the composite index. Fig. 4.5 describes the spatial evolution of the index within the Italian context (arrows represent increasing levels of land vulnerability).

Increasing levels of land vulnerability have been detected in dry areas of Southern regions (major islands and the plain known as "Tavoliere delle Puglie," located in Apulia region). This negative framework mainly arises from improper land management, increasing land-use intensity (especially in the agricultural sector), demographic pressure, and degradation of biophysical resources Finally, a newly designed synthetic index (the so-called DSI) may support the estimate of agricultural drought through a simplified water balance approach, evaluating the intensity of dryness in periods of limited

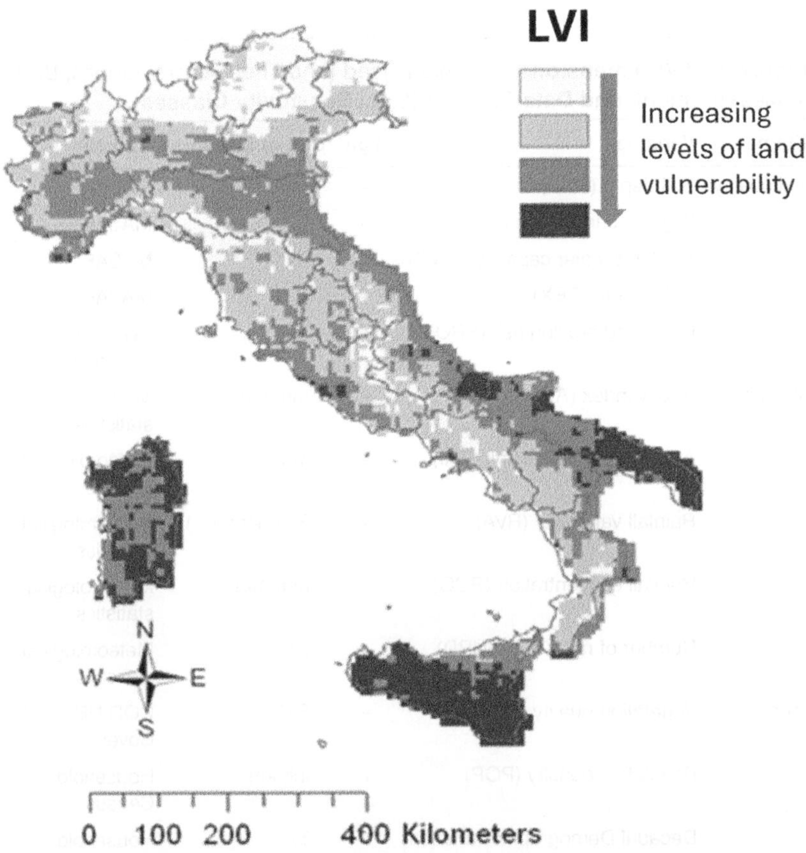

Fig. 4.5 LVI Distribution in Italy for the Year 2000, with Darker Colors Indicating Greater Land Vulnerability Contribution of the LVI in 2000 over Italy: Darker Colors Indicate Higher Land Vulnerability Levels.
Source: Authors' Elaboration of Official Statistics.

rainfall. The index implementation only adopts daily estimates of rainfall and temperature as input variables, thus encouraging its adoption in case of low availability of agriculture-related meteorological data (e.g., Motha & Sivakumar, 2001).

In general, DSI yields a drought estimate that is broadly consistent with values derived from more comprehensive and integrated indices, such as SPI (Standardized Precipitation Index) and DRI (Drought Reconnaissance Index). The proposed methodology thus allows for the inherent representation of complex climatic interactions associated with drought events in a single value for a specific time period (Incerti et al., 2007). Therefore, the temporal profile of the DSI not only provides information dealing with drought risk during a given period, but also regarding the duration and persistence of the phenomenon over time (Salvati et al., 2009). In the final stage, the three modules are fully integrated into a GIS environment, allowing the proposed indices to provide a more comprehensive and detailed evaluation of drought dynamics.

POLICY-MAKERS RECOMMENDATIONS

The above strategies suggest an integrated approach to drought monitoring. At the river-basin level, further investigation of drought patterns will require accurate analysis enabling conservation, maintenance, and mitigation actions to be taken to ensure effective protection of the territory. The involvement of local stakeholders is essential for managing soil cover, from planting in erosion-prone areas to implementing sustainable silvicultural practices, which require the constant commitment of farmers and foresters. Rural communities can fulfill these tasks if they are well guided and supported and, above all, if their essential role in safeguarding the territory is recognized and encouraged. This requires creating favorable conditions for their settlement processes, including new employment opportunities, especially for younger generations, who could return to oversee the territory by combining specialized and "niche" productions. However, financial incentives should be provided for future farmers to compensate for low agricultural income and as remuneration for their work in protecting the land (Jakubínský et al. 2021; Salvati et al. 2015; Salvati et al. 2009b).

The necessary public expenditure could be partly financed through rural development aid from the European Union and partly through the elimination of compensation mechanisms for mitigating damage caused by natural hazards. Similarly, the proposed strategies require the integration of different information layers. In line with recent trends that suggest evaluating drought events through the simultaneous use of different parameters or indices (Wu & Wilhite, 2004), the scheme described was applied using a composite LVI. Indeed, complex methods for assessing drought conditions require a comprehensive framework that combines various aspects (Svoboda et al., 2002), covering (a) climate and hydro-meteorological indicators, (b) soil and topographic characteristics, (c) vegetation and land cover conditions, and (d) human factors, such as land use, population dynamics, urbanization, and tourism pressure.

CONCLUDING REMARKS

Protecting social and economic heritage, as well as natural capital at large, is a crucial responsibility of decision-makers. Such a protection level should be grounded in effective policies for soil conservation and integrated water resource management. Existing policies should reconcile the development of new industrial, urban, and tourist facilities with the implementation of incentive systems to revitalize rural areas and marginal territories. Soil protection and water resource management should involve experts, local stakeholders, research centers, and citizens to achieve rational land-use planning through appropriate operational decisions.

Areas destined to irrigated crops should be incorporated into land-use planning, as irrigated land strongly influences watershed behavior. The design of river basin plans implies considering the availability of water resources and their allocation among different sections, namely irrigation, drinking water, and other applications. This information dataset should include assessments of water use efficiency in agriculture, drainage in irrigated regions, crop irrigation requirements, and groundwater withdrawals. Moving toward a holistic assessment of drought risk, the above-described indices (DSI and LVI) implicitly prioritize the most vulnerable areas, thereby facilitating the work of policy-makers responsible for implementing prevention, mitigation, and environmental recovery policies.

REFERENCES

Armanini, A. (1999). *Previsione e prevenzione del rischio da colata di detriti.* Atti Convegni Lincei. Il rischio idrogeologico e la difesa del suolo: 13–44.

Baldi, G., Di Lotto, P., & Frassani, A. (1994). *Strumenti di supporto ai piani di bacino*. Prima monografia sulla difesa del suolo. Ed. CNR/CNDS: 86-148.

Biasi, R., Brunori, E., Ferrara, C., & Salvati, L. (2019). Assessing impacts of climate change on phenology and quality traits of Vitis vinifera L.: The contribution of local knowledge. *Plants*, *8*(5), 121.

Canfora, L., Salvati, L., Benedetti, A., & Francaviglia, R. (2017). Is soil microbial diversity affected by soil and groundwater salinity? Evidences from a coastal system in central Italy. *Environmental Monitoring and Assessment*, *189*, 1–15.

Cicco, N., Candido, V., Coluzzi, R., Imbrenda, V., Lanfredi, M., Larocca, M., Lorusso, A., Benelli, C., & Sofo, A. (2025). Revitalizing marginal areas of Basilicata (Southern Italy) with saffron: A strategy approach mixing alternative cultivation system and land suitability analysis. *Land*, *14*(4), 902. https://doi.org/10.3390/land14040902

Cillis, G., Coluzzi, R., Salvati, L., Colantoni, A., Nosava, B., Imbrenda, V., & Lanfredi, M. (2025). Water resource management in tourism hotspot: A cost-effective, semi-automatic method for monitoring the diffusion of residential swimming pools. *Ecological Informatics*, 103333.

Colantoni, A., Ferrara, C., Perini, L., & Salvati, L. (2015). Assessing trends in climate aridity and vulnerability to soil degradation in Italy. *Ecological Indicators*, *48*, 599–604.

Coluzzi, R., Perrone, A., Samela, C., Imbrenda, V., Manfreda, S., Pace, L., & Lanfredi, M. (2025). Rapid landslide detection from free optical satellite imagery using a robust change detection technique. *Scientific Reports*, *15*(1), 4697. https://doi.org/10.1038/s41598-025-89542-8

De Wrachien, D., & Ragab, R. (2003). *Variabilità climatica e suo impatto sul bilancio disponibilità idriche e fabbisogni irrigui nel bacino del Mediterraneo*. Atti del Congresso Internazionale ANBI-FAO, Roma: 77–97.

Egidi, G., Salvati, L., & Vinci, S. (2020). The long way to tipperary: City size and worldwide urban population trends, 1950–2030. *Sustainable Cities and Society*, *60*, 102148.

Ferrara, C., Carlucci, M., Grigoriadis, E., Corona, P., & Salvati, L. (2017). A comprehensive insight into the geography of forest cover in Italy: Exploring the importance of socioeconomic local contexts. *Forest Policy and Economics*, *75*, 12–22.

Ferrara, A., Kelly, C., Wilson, G. A., Nolè, A., Mancino, G., Bajocco, S., & Salvati, L. (2016). Shaping the role of 'fast' and 'slow' drivers of change in forest-shrubland socio-ecological systems. *Journal of Environmental Management*, *169*, 155–166.

Ferrara, A., Kosmas, C., Salvati, L., Padula, A., Mancino, G., & Nolè, A. (2020). Updating the MEDALUS-ESA framework for worldwide land degradation and desertification assessment. *Land Degradation & Development, 31*(12), 1593–1607.

Francaviglia, R., Di Bene, C., Farina, R., Salvati, L., & Vicente-Vicente, J. L. (2019). Assessing "4 per 1000" soil organic carbon storage rates under Mediterranean climate: A comprehensive data analysis. *Mitigation and Adaptation Strategies for Global Change, 24*, 795–818.

Imbrenda, V., D'Emilio, M., Lanfredi, M., Ragosta, M., & Simoniello, T. (2013). Indicators of land degradation vulnerability due to anthropic factors: Tools for an efficient planning. In G.Borruso., S.Bertazzon., A.Favretto., B.Murgante., & C.M.Torre. *Geographic information analysis for sustainable development and economic planning: New technologies* (pp. 87–101). IGI Global.

Imbrenda, V., Gómez, C. M., D'Emilio, M., Samela, C., Salvati, L., Matarazzo, N., Lanfredi, M., Coluzzi, R. (2023). Remote sensing and spatial databases for investigating latent urban-rural dynamics in rural, inland districts of Southern Italy. *Cuadernos de investigación geográfica: Geographical Research Letters, 49*(2), 143–162.

Incerti, G., Feoli, E., Salvati, L., Brunetti, A., & Giovacchini, A. (2007). Analysis of bioclimatic time series and their neural network-based classification to characterise drought risk patterns in South Italy. *International Journal of Biometeorology, 51*(4), 253–263. https://doi.org/10.1007/s00484-006-0071-6

ISTAT. (2003). *Censimento Generale dell'Agricoltura.* ISTAT.

Jakubínský, J., Prokopová, M., Raška, P., Salvati, L., Bezak, N., Cudlín, O., Cudlín, P., Purkyt, J., Vezza, P., Camporeale, C., Daněk, J., Pástor, M., & Lepeška, T. (2021). Managing floodplains using nature-based solutions to support multiple ecosystem functions and services. *Wiley Interdisciplinary Reviews: Water, 8*(5), e1545.

Kairis, O., Kosmas, C., Karavitis, C., Ritsema, C., Salvati, L., Acikalin, S., Alcalá, M., Alfama, P., Atlhopheng, J., Barrera, J., Belgacem, A., Solé-Benet, A., Brito, J., Chaker, M., Chanda, R., Coelho, C., Darkoh, M., Diamantis, I., Ermolaeva, O., Fassouli, V., ... Ziogas, A. (2014). Evaluation and selection of indicators for land degradation and desertification monitoring: types of degradation, causes, and implications for management. *Environmental Management, 54*, 971–982.

Kosmas, C., Kairis, O., Karavitis, C., Acikalin, S., Alcalá, M., Alfama, P., Atlhopheng, J., Barrera, J., Belgacem, A., Solé-Benet, A., Brito, J., Chaker, M., Chanda, R., Darkoh, M., Ermolaeva, O., Fassouli, V., Fernandez, F., Gokceoglu, C., Gonzalez, D., ... Salvati, L. (2015). An exploratory analysis of land abandonment drivers in areas prone to desertification. *Catena, 128*, 252–261.

Lanfredi, M., Coluzzi, R., Imbrenda, V., Macchiato, M., & Simoniello, T. (2020). Analyzing space–time coherence in precipitation seasonality across different European climates. *Remote Sensing, 12*(1), 171. https://doi.org/10.3390/rs12010171

Leone, A. (2004). *Ambiente e territorio agroforestale*. Franco Angeli.

Ligetvari, F., & Szalai, S. (2004). Monitoring of drought development case study for the year 2003. In *Proceedings of ICID Interregional Conference on Food Production and Water*, Moscow, Russia.

Mancino, G., Nolè, A., Salvati, L., & Ferrara, A. (2016). In-between forest expansion and cropland decline: A revised USLE model for soil erosion risk under land-use change in a Mediterranean region. *Ecological Indicators, 71*, 544–550.

Motha, R. P., & Sivakumar, M. V. K. (2001). Software for agroclimatic data management. *Proceedings of an Expert Group Meeting*, Washington, DC, USA, 16–20 October 2000. Staff Report WAOB-2001-2; 194 pages.

Pace, L., Imbrenda, V., Lanfredi, M., Cudlín, P., Simoniello, T., Salvati, L., & Coluzzi, R. (2023). Delineating the intrinsic, long-term path of land degradation: A spatially explicit transition matrix for Italy, 1960–2010. *International Journal of Environmental Research and Public Health, 20*(3), 2402. https://doi.org/10.3390/ijerph20032402

Passino, R. (2002). *Le strategie di intervento nei grandi bacini fluviali*. Atti Convegni Lincei. Il dissesto idrogeologico, pp. 221–226.

Perini, L. (2004). Atlante agroclimatico. *P.F. Climagri*. Ministero per le Politiche Agricole e Forestali, Linea di ricerca 2.1, Roma.

Preti, F. (2002). *Quantificazione degli effetti delle evoluzioni territoriali sui deflussi di piena di un bacino agricolo forestale*. Atti Convegni Lincei. Il dissesto idrogeologico: inventario e prospettive: 467–478.

Puglisi, S. (2002). *Dal consolidamento alla rinaturazione dei versanti*. Atti Convegni Lincei. Il dissesto idrogeologico: inventario e prospettive, pp. 147–163.

Quaranta, G., Salvia, R., Salvati, L., Paola, V. D., Coluzzi, R., Imbrenda, V., & Simoniello, T. (2020). Long-term impacts of grazing management on land degradation in a rural community of Southern Italy: Depopulation matters. *Land Degradation & Development*, *31*(16), 2379–2394. https://doi.org/10.1002/ldr.3583

Ragosta, M., Daniele, G., Imbrenda, V., Coluzzi, R., D'Emilio, M., Lanfredi, M., & Matarazzo, N. (2024). Land Transformations in Irpinia (Southern Italy): A tale on the socio-economic dynamics acting in a marginal area of the Mediterranean Europe. *Sustainability*, *16*(19), 8724.

Sallustio, L., Pettenella, D., Merlini, P., Romano, R., Salvati, L., Marchetti, M., & Corona, P. (2018). Assessing the economic marginality of agricultural lands in Italy to support land use planning. *Land Use Policy*, *76*, 526–534.

Salvati, L. (2013). Monitoring high-quality soil consumption driven by urban pressure in a growing city (Rome, Italy). *Cities*, *31*, 349–356.

Salvati, L., & Carlucci, M. (2014). A composite index of sustainable development at the local scale: Italy as a case study. *Ecological Indicators*, *43*, 162–171.

Salvati, L., & Zitti, M. (2005). Land degradation in the Mediterranean basin: Linking bio-physical and economic factors into an ecological perspective. *Biota*, *6*, 67–77.

Salvati, L., & Zitti, M. (2008). Regional convergence of environmental variables: empirical evidences from land degradation. *Ecological Economics*, *68*(1–2), 162–168.

Salvati, L., & Zitti, M. (2009). Substitutability and weighting of ecological and economic indicators: Exploring the importance of various components of a synthetic index. *Ecological Economics*, *68*(4), 1093–1099.

Salvati, L., Bajocco, S., Ceccarelli, T., Zitti, M., & Perini, L. (2011). Towards a process-based evaluation of land vulnerability to soil degradation in Italy. *Ecological Indicators*, *11*(5), 1216–1227.

Salvati, L., Mavrakis, A., Colantoni, A., Mancino, G., & Ferrara, A. (2015). Complex Adaptive Systems, soil degradation and land sensitivity to desertification: A multivariate assessment of Italian agro-forest landscape. *Science of the Total Environment*, *521*, 235–245.

Salvati, L., Perini, L., Sabbi, A., & Bajocco, S. (2012). Climate aridity and land use changes: A regional-scale analysis. *Geographical Research*, *50*(2), 193–203.

Salvati, L., Petitta, M., Ceccarelli, T., Perini, L., Di Battista, F., Scarascia, M. E. V. (2008). Italy's renewable water resources as estimated on the basis of the monthly water balance. *Irrigation and Drainage*, *57*(5), 507–515.

Salvati, L., Scarascia, M. E. V., & Zitti, M. (2009). Monitoring drought severity in agriculture through a synthetic index based on dry periods: A case study in the Mediterranean basin. *Irrigation and Drainage*, *58*(5), 596–606. https://doi.org/10.1002/ird.441

Salvati, L., Zitti, M., & Ceccarelli, T. (2008). Integrating economic and environmental indicators in the assessment of desertification risk: A case study. *Applied Ecological and Environmental Research*, *6*(1), 129–138.

Salvati, L., Zitti, M., Ceccarelli, T., & Perini, L. (2009b). Developinga synthetic index of land vulnerability to drought and desertification. *Geographical Research*, *47*(3), 280–291. https://doi.org/10.1111/j.1745-5871.2009.00590.x

Scarascia, M. E. V., Battista, F. D., & Salvati, L. (2006). Water resources in Italy: Availability and agricultural uses. *Irrigation and Drainage*, *55*(2), 115–127. https://doi.org/10.1002/ird.222

Seifollahi-Aghmiuni, S., Kalantari, Z., Egidi, G., Gaburova, L., & Salvati, L. (2022). Urbanisation-driven land degradation and socioeconomic challenges in peri-urban areas: Insights from Southern Europe. *Ambio*, *51*(6), 1446–1458.

Svoboda, M., LeComte, D., Hayes, M., Heim, R., Gleason, K., Angel, J., Rippey, B., Tinker, R., Palecki, M., Stooksbury, D., Miskus, D., & Stephens, S. (2002). The drought monitor. *Bulletin of the American Meteorological Society*, *83*(8), 1181–1190. https://doi.org/10.1175/1520-0477-83.8.1181

Tomao, A., Quatrini, V., Corona, P., Ferrara, A., Lafortezza, R., & Salvati, L. (2017). Resilient landscapes in Mediterranean urban areas: Understanding factors influencing forest trends. *Environmental Research*, *156*, 1–9.

Ugolini, M., & Mordini, L. (2002). *I progetti di riqualificazione ambientale per la tutela del paesaggio montano. Conoscenza dell'ambiente e rischio idrogeologico*. Atti Convegno Nazionale CNR, IRPI, GNDCI. Conservazione dell'ambiente e rischio idrogeologico, pp. 695–706.

Wilson, G. A., Kelly, C. L., Briassoulis, H., Ferrara, A., Quaranta, G., Salvia, R., Detsis, V., Curfs, M., Cerda, A., El-Aich, A., Liu, H., Kosmas, C., Alados, C. L., Imeson, A., Landgrebe-Trinkunaite, R., Salvati, L.,

Naumann, S., Danwen, H., Iosifides, T., ... Zhang, P. (2017). Social memory and the resilience of communities affected by land degradation. *Land Degradation & Development*, *28*(2), 383–400.

Wu, H., & Wilhite, D. A. (2004). An operational agricultural drought risk assessment model for Nebraska, USA. *Natural Hazards*, *33*(1), 1–21. https://doi.org/10.1023/B:NHAZ.0000034994.44357.75

5

OPTIMAL RESOURCE MANAGEMENT AND THE "LANDSCAPE NEXUS": ENVISIONING AND COMMUNICATING SOCIAL COMPLEXITY

ALESSIA D'AGATA[a], MAURIZIO MASI[b], LUIGI FICI[b], MARCO MAIALETTI[c], DONATO SCARPITTA[d], BOGDANA NOSOVA[e], IOANNIS KONAXIS[f] AND LUCA SALVATI[a]

[a]*Sapienza University of Rome, Italy*
[b]*Tuscia University, Italy*
[c]*Independent Researcher and Lawyer, Rome, Italy*
[d]*Independent Research and Architect, Salerno, Italy*
[e]*Taras Shevchenko National University of Kyiv, Ukraine*
[f]*University of Piraeus, Greece*

ABSTRACT

This chapter aims at designing strategies and measures to combat land degradation (LD), looking at the territorial specificities, and delineating the more relevant trajectories of change over time. Policies against social inequalities, particularly in rural and peripheral areas, are revealed as critical to mitigate risk in areas vulnerable to LD. This issue should also imply a joint active collaboration between all relevant stakeholders, in designing strategic measures against LD. To this purpose, notable examples support the contextualization of the phenomenon and its impact on policy decisions. The rapid evolution of ecological and socioeconomic conditions sharply affects environmental sensitivity and landscape degradation.

Within this framework, Italy is recognized as a hotspot of LD, due to its recurring experience of the combined effects of soil degradation, significant land-use changes, anthropogenic pressure, and climate change. The work follows the ESA (Environmentally Sensitive Areas) methodology classifying Italy into different levels of vulnerability to LD between 1960 and 2020.

Keywords: Land degradation climate scenarios sustainability indicators Italy

INTRODUCTION

Economic progress and industrial development, particularly in more developed countries, have been mainly achieved using frameworks promoting a wide and often uncontrolled exploitation of natural resources (Seifollahi-Aghmiuni et al., 2022; Tomao et al., 2017; Wilson et al., 2017). These models focus on a truly anthropocentric vision of the relationship between man and the environment, derived from a biased interpretation of the principle of supremacy of the human being over nature (Egidi et al., 2020; Sallustio et al., 2018; Salvati & Carlucci, 2014). Within this context, environment has been considered an unexhaustive resource, aimed at satisfying economic and social needs, without a proper consideration of the ecological limitations and the long-term implications of territorial transformations (Salvati & Zitti, 2008).

Starting from the 1970s, an alternative theoretical framework began to establish, being able to recognize the complexity and multiplicity of the relationships between social and natural ecosystems (Salvati et al., 2008). This novel approach progressively challenged the traditional conceptual separation between society and environment, thus highlighting the crucial impact of biophysical factors on the organization of human societies, along with that of anthropogenic activities on ecological equilibriums (Beato, 1998). The resulting dynamic and integrated vision acknowledges the bidirectional relationship between nature and society (Quaranta et al., 2020).

Within this context, the development of the environmental movement, inspired by the theories of Catton and Dunlap, introduces the concept of "environmental carrying capacity" in any socioeconomic evaluation (Ferrara et al., 2016). This concept remarks the undeniable subordination of human communities to the limitations dictated by environmental conditions, and the inescapable constraints of ecology, highlighting the unsustainability of development models neglecting such structural constraints (Beato, 1999).

The "environmental carrying capacity" then becomes a crucial interpretative tool to understand the processes of territorial transformation and their environmental implications (Salvati et al., 2015). Moreover, the so-called "ecological paradigm" reinforces this perspective, highlighting the necessity of a systemic organization and a reflexive interplay between scientific knowledge and ethics (Morin, 1973). Within this framework, ecology emerges as the first discipline to explicitly shape the relationship between humanity and nature, recognizing the human being as integrating part of natural systems rather than their dominator (Salvati & Zitti, 2005). This perspective strongly supports the challenges arising from environmental sustainability and the responsible management of territorial resources. Specifically, LD acquires a paradigmatic role in the interaction between man and the environment, constituting the main threat to environmental sustainability (Salvati & Zitti, 2009), affecting the ecosystems productivity, food security and ability of territories to respond to environmental and socioeconomic pressures (Fig. 5.1).

The present work studies these dynamics by means of several territorial indicators, aimed at achieving an integrated evaluation of the vulnerability to LD at national and regional levels (e.g., Ferrara et al., 2017). It explores the main issues connected with the development of an interpretative framework integrating environmental sustainability and LD processes (e.g., Kairis et al., 2014).

Fig. 5.1 Natural Environments Exposed to Physical Degradation.
Source: Authors' Photographic Archive.

The analyzed time horizon extends between 1960 and the present time, highlighting long-term transformations and significant trends in the relationship between human activities and territorial systems.

METHODOLOGY

The analysis has been performed at the national level using the Environmentally Sensitive Areas (ESA) model, estimating the territorial vulnerability to LD on the basis of four components (Kosmas et al., 2015): climate, soil, vegetation, and land management (Fig. 5.2). The temporal evolution of LD has been studied dividing the analyzed period into 10-year sub-periods and relies on four thematic indices jointly defining the Environmentally Sensitive Areas Index (ESAI), i.e., the Climate Quality Indicator (CQI), the Soil Quality Indicator (SQI), the Vegetation Quality Indicator (VQI) and the Land Management and Human Pressure Quality Indicator (MQI). The first indicator, CQI, computed for years 1951 to 2010, combines the mean annual precipitation, the aridity index (computed as precipitation-to-evapotranspiration ratio) and the compass orientation of a terrain surface (aspect). Its design relies on the meteorological data (temperature, rainfall, solar radiation, humidity, and wind) retrieved in a meteorological database interpolated on a national georeferenced grid of 544 points (Incerti et al., 2007).

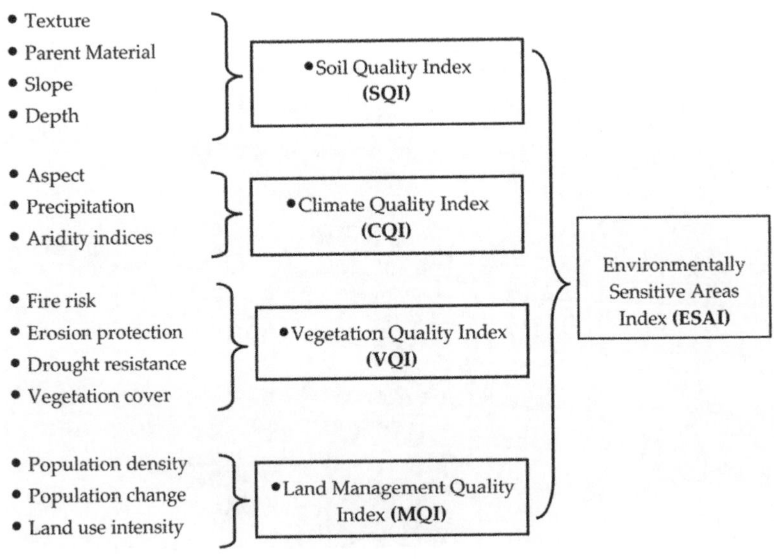

Fig. 5.2 Variables Used in the ESA Model.
Source: Authors' Elaboration of Recent Literature.

Moreover, SQI was derived from the soil layer map developed under the DISMED (Desertification Information System to Support National Action Programs in the Mediterranean) project and relies on the European Soil Database with a resolution of 1 km^2 (Joint Research Center, ISPRA – Italian Institute for Environmental Protection and Research). The analyzed time span suggests a static approach to its determinants, i.e., depth, texture, slope, and parent material (Salvati & Bajocco, 2011; Salvati et al., 2011).

VQI relies on the databases including the Land Use Map of Italy (LUM60) and the different CORINE Land Cover (CLC) from 1990 to 2012. It considers data on vegetation cover, fire risk, protection against erosion and drought resistance of the studied area, depending on its vegetation peculiarities. Finally, the MQI is a function of population density based on census data aggregated at municipal level. Data on its annual growth rate can be retrieved from official statistics, namely ISTAT (Italian National Institute of Statistics) databases (Salvati, 2013). The combination of these four environmental quality indicators, computed as the geometric mean of the related four values, provides the composite index of vulnerability of the territory, the so-called ESAI. ESAI is scaled from 1, representing low vulnerability, to 2, representing high vulnerability of a given place (Colantoni et al., 2015; Ferrara et al., 2020; Salvati et al., 2012). Starting from each analyzed unit, results were aggregated at the level of administrative regions (i.e., NUTS2 level – Nomenclature of Territorial Units for official Statistics, Eurostat) and country (i.e., NUTS1 level).

RESULTS

For Italy, the average value of the ESAI over the analyzed period increased from 1.34 to about 1.37, reporting an average annual positive variation of approximately 0.03%. ESAI growth only partially affects the national territory, mainly focusing on local peculiarities. Examples of deteriorating health conditions could be provided by the Adriatic coastline and the Po Valley, registering significant positive variations. On contrary, negligible or stable levels of vulnerability have been observed for mountainous areas, particularly the Eastern Alps and the Central-Northern Apennines, as well as Southern Italy which, despite recording the highest ESAI values, showed fairly limited variations over time. The diachronic analysis conducted at the regional scale provides further insights into the spatial heterogeneity of the ESAI (Table 5.1).

To track the evolution of LD vulnerability, the average ESAI values were shown at three specific years (1960, 1990, 2010) reporting, in brackets, the position of each region within the national ranking of vulnerability to LD.

Table 5.1 Average ESAI Value in the Italian Regions in the Years 1960, 1990, 2010 (Position of Each Region in the Final Vulnerability Ranking) and Annual Rate of Change, 1960–2010.

Administrative Region	ESAI Value (Rank)			% Change
	1960	1990	2010	
Sicily	1.434(1)	1.427(2)	1.431(1)	0.00
Apulia	1.391(2)	1.428(1)	1.404(2)	0.02
Basilicata	1.370(3)	1.384(4)	1.383(5)	0.02
Sardinia	1.367(4)	1.377(5)	1.387(4)	0.03
Molise	1.359(5)	1.384(3)	1.361(6)	0.00
Emilia-Romagna	1.345(6)	1.370(6)	1.390(3)	0.07
Abruzzo	1.338(7)	1.360(9)	1.325(15)	–0.02
Lazio	1.338(8)	1.351(10)	1.357(12)	0.03
Campania	1.338(9)	1.361(8)	1.360(11)	0.03
Marche	1.332(10)	1.365(7)	1.369(8)	0.06
Tuscany	1.331(11)	1.338(14)	1.361(10)	0.05
Lombardy	1.326(12)	1.340(13)	1.369(7)	0.07
Calabria	1.326(13)	1.342(12)	1.334(13)	0.01
Veneto	1.321(14)	1.347(11)	1.367(9)	0.07
Piemonte	1.315(15)	1.319(15)	1.331(14)	0.03
Liguria	1.314(16)	1.300(17)	1.313(17)	0.00
Umbria	1.296(17)	1.309(16)	1.318(16)	0.03
Friuli-Venezia Giulia	1.294(18)	1.296(18)	1.304(18)	0.01
Aosta Valley	1.289(19)	1.270(19)	1.301(19)	0.02
Trentino-Alto Adige	1.273(20)	1.262(20)	1.291(20)	0.03

Data highlight that, over time, the ranking of some regions has experienced significant fluctuations. Nevertheless, Sicily and Apulia stabilized in the top positions, exhibiting a high percentage of areas affected by severe vulnerability to LD. In 1960, the third position of Basilicata (Southern Italy), then falling to fifth place, was occupied by Emilia Romagna in 2010, which had previously ranked sixth. In general, Northern regions exhibited greater ESAI increases compared with Southern regions which, on the contrary, had higher overall ESAI scores. In terms of surface area, the areas least affected by soil degradation (prevalently inland mountainous districts in both the North and Central Italy) have remained almost stable over time.

At national level, there has been a significant increase of the areas characterized by critical ESAI values, increasing from 33% of the territory in 1960 to 47% in 2010. The most significant changes occurred in the North

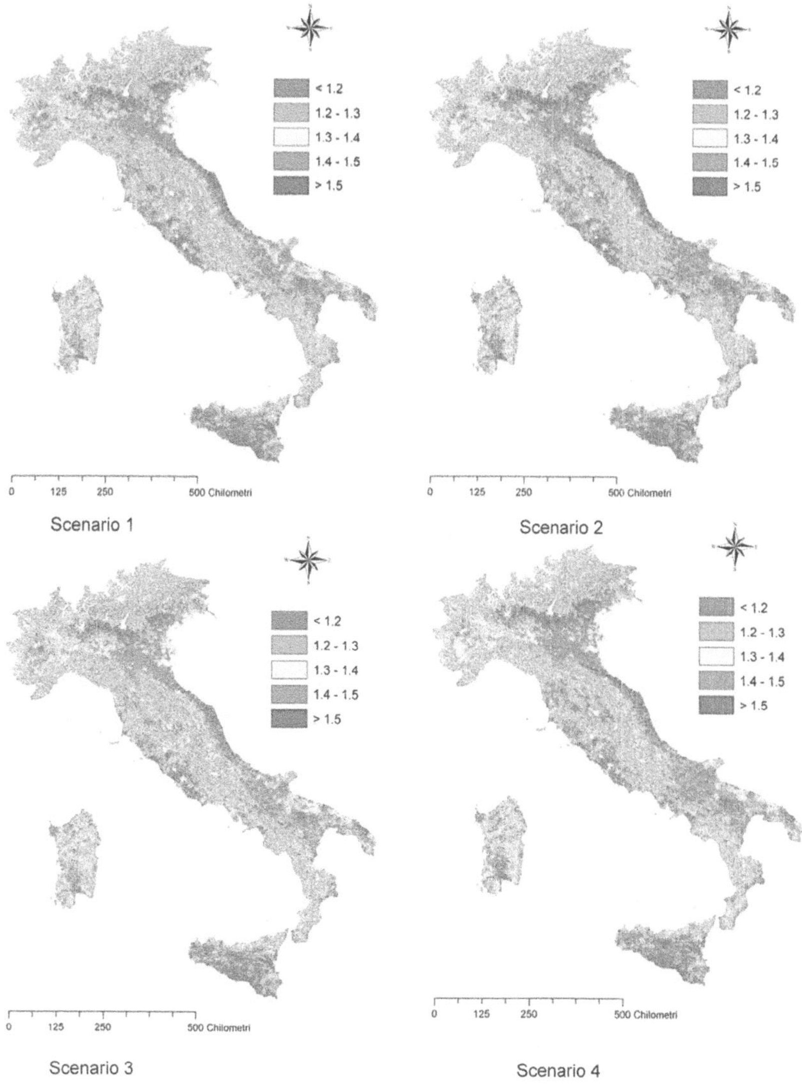

Fig. 5.3. ESAI Trends in Italy According to the Four Reference Scenarios.

(+20%) and the Center (+16%), while the increase in the South (+7%) was rather limited. ESAI trends for 2020 were analyzed under four scenarios (S1–S4), as presented in Fig. 5.3 (Perini et al., 2007), being connected with a fixed growth of the average annual temperature, compared to the reference climatic averages 1961–1990, and two distinctive demographic dynamics, one assuming population stability, the other establishing the same rate of demographic growth observed between 2000 and 2010 (Table 5.2).

Table 5.2 Climate Change Scenarios for 2020.

Scenario	Temperature Increase		Demographic Dynamics	
	+0.3 °C	+0.7 °C	Stable	Increasing
S1	•		•	
S2		•	•	
S3	•			•
S4		•		•

Temperature increases predicted by the above scenarios represent a conservative estimate of climate change compared with estimates resulting from deterministic models. As expected from the initial assumption, the most critical scenario was S4, in which a higher temperature increase is combined with a greater anthropogenic pressure, whose effects contribute to an overall higher vulnerability to LD. Nevertheless, the different geographical areas perform peculiar responses. In particular, the greater increase in the ESAI highlighted by scenario S4 mainly refers to Central and Southern regions, except for the major islands, whose results are coherent with the previously discussed trends. In general, a generalized deterioration of environmental conditions was observed, even in the least problematic scenarios.

DISCUSSION

The findings presented in this work reveal the complexity of LD processes in Italy, highlighting geographical heterogeneity reflected in environmental factors and local socioeconomic pressures (Andersson et al., 2011; Barbier & Hochard, 2018; Pani, 2020, Carlucci et al., 2022). Despite the persisting relevance of physical and biological factors, LD territorial trajectories have been increasingly affected by anthropogenic dynamics, including land-use dynamics, demographic trends, and governance quality (Imbrenda et al., 2022; Salvati & Zitti, 2009, Salvati et al., 2009). Further evidence derives from the uneven distribution of degradation levels in Northern Italy, particularly in peri-urban areas, indicating that the traditional urban–rural dichotomy is displaced by the type of local development and specific spatial interdependencies of settlements and rural districts (Coluzzi et al., 2022; Imbrenda et al., 2023, 2024).

Regional variations in the ESAI further highlight the need for territorially diversified policy solutions, tailored to the specific environmental sensitivity and each region's institutional capacity (Mancino et al., 2016). Although the historically recorded higher ESAI scores registered in Southern regions, their persisting stability can be attributed to a combination of saturation, degradation processes and a certain resilience associated with land abandonment, reforestation or rural depopulation (Cicco et al., 2025; Cudlín et al., 2021; Gül & Esen, 2024; Matarazzo et al., 2025; Pace et al., 2023; Ragosta et al., 2024; Rajbanshi & Das, 2021). Conversely, the acceleration of vulnerability in the North remarked the socio-ecological imbalances associated with urban expansion, infrastructure pressure and intensified land consumption.

Effective policy frameworks should promote coordination at multiple scales along with environmental protection, social equity, and economic development (Chasek et al., 2019; Halbac-Cotoara-Zamfir et al., 2020; Sklenicka et al., 2020). Future scenarios highlight the (potential) combined risks of climate variability and demographic growth. Specifically, in scenario S4, the synergic interaction between rising temperatures and population growth exacerbates vulnerability to LD at the local level, as already observed in specialized agricultural systems (e.g., Biasi et al., 2019). Adaptation strategies should consider both mitigation and demographic transition policies involving local stakeholders to incorporate locally based knowledge systems (Canfora et al., 2017; Francaviglia et al., 2019; Metternicht et al., 2019).

CONCLUDING REMARKS

Recently observed higher rate of increase in ESAI values can be partially connected to the socioeconomic conditions fueled by growing levels of urbanization. The significant growth of this index in Northern Italy, characterized by a patchy distribution, highlights the effects of urban and peri-urban expansion of large cities (e.g., Milan and Turin) subject to significant anthropogenic pressure, generally extending proportionally and radially to neighboring rural areas. These considerations highlight the opportunity and urgency of preparing countermeasures/strategies to capture territorial peculiarities (Briassoulis, 2011) as well as better delineating the trajectories of change over time (Wilson & Juntti, 2005). The development of policies to address social disparities, notably in rural and peripheral regions, is vital to mitigate ecological risk in areas vulnerable to LD (Jakubínský et al., 2021). In local districts respecting principles of social equity, it is indeed possible to foster a culture of environmental protection and enhancement, as well as to successfully involving all stakeholders in the strategic planning of measures to face land degradation more appropriately.

REFERENCES

Andersson, E., Brogaard, S., & Olsson, L. (2011). The political ecology of land degradation. *Annual Review of Environment and Resources*, *36*(1), 295–319. https://doi.org/10.1146/annurev-environ-033110-092827

Barbier, E. B., & Hochard, J. P. (2018). Land degradation and poverty. *Nature Sustainability*, *1*(11), 623–631. https://doi.org/10.1038/s41893-018-0155-4

Beato, F. (1998). *Rischio e mutamento ambientale globale*. Percorsi di sociologia dell'ambiente, Milano, Franco Angeli.

Beato, F. (1999). *Parchi e società*. Turismo sostenibile e sistemi locali, Napoli, Liguori.

Biasi, R., Brunori, E., Ferrara, C., & Salvati, L. (2019). Assessing impacts of climate change on phenology and quality traits of Vitis vinifera L.: The contribution of local knowledge. *Plants*, *8*(5), 121.

Briassoulis, H. (2011). Governing desertification in Mediterranean Europe: The challenge of environmental policy integration in multi-level governance contexts. *Land Degradation & Development*, 22(3), 313–325. https://doi.org/10.1002/ldr.1018

Canfora, L., Salvati, L., Benedetti, A., & Francaviglia, R. (2017). Is soil microbial diversity affected by soil and groundwater salinity? Evidences from a coastal system in central Italy. *Environmental Monitoring and Assessment*, *189*, 1–15.

Carlucci, M., Salvia, R., Quaranta, G., Salvati, L., & Imbrenda, V. (2022). Official statistics, spatio-temporal dynamics and local-scale monitoring: Toward integrated environmental-economic accounting for land degradation. *Letters in Spatial and Resource Sciences*, *15*(3), 469–491. https://doi.org/10.1007/s12076-022-00319-y.

Chasek, P., Akhtar-Schuster, M., Orr, B. J., Luise, A., Rakoto Ratsimba, H., & Safriel, U. (2019). Land degradation neutrality: The science-policy interface from the UNCCD to national implementation. *Environmental Science & Policy*, 92, 182–190. https://doi.org/10.1016/j.envsci.2018.11.017

Cicco, N., Candido, V., Coluzzi, R., Imbrenda, V., Lanfredi, M., Larocca, M., Lorusso, A., Benelli, C., & Sofo, A. (2025). Revitalizing marginal areas of Basilicata (Southern Italy) with Saffron: A strategy approach mixing alternative cultivation system and land suitability analysis. *Land*, *14*(4), 902. https://doi.org/10.3390/land14040902

Colantoni, A., Ferrara, C., Perini, L., & Salvati, L. (2015). Assessing trends in climate aridity and vulnerability to soil degradation in Italy. *Ecological Indicators*, *48*, 599–604.

Coluzzi, R., Bianchini, L., Egidi, G., Cudlin, P., Imbrenda, V., Salvati, L., & Lanfredi, M. (2022). Density matters? Settlement expansion and land degradation in Peri-urban and rural districts of Italy. *Environmental impact assessment review*, *92*, 106703. https://doi.org/10.1016/j.eiar.2021.106703

Cudlín, O., Pechanec, V., Prokopová, M., & Cudlín, P. (2021). Assessing the vulnerability to land degradation of (not only) rural landscapes using the ESAI Index. *Journal of Landscape Ecology*, *14*(3), 128–144. https://doi.org/10.2478/jlecol-2021-0020

Egidi, G., Salvati, L., & Vinci, S. (2020). The long way to tipperary: City size and worldwide urban population trends, 1950–2030. *Sustainable Cities and Society*, *60*, 102148.

Ferrara, C., Carlucci, M., Grigoriadis, E., Corona, P., & Salvati, L. (2017). A comprehensive insight into the geography of forest cover in Italy: Exploring the importance of socioeconomic local contexts. *Forest Policy and Economics*, *75*, 12–22.

Ferrara, A., Kelly, C., Wilson, G. A., Nolè, A., Mancino, G., Bajocco, S., & Salvati, L. (2016). Shaping the role of 'fast' and 'slow' drivers of change in forest-shrubland socio-ecological systems. *Journal of Environmental Management*, *169*, 155–166.

Ferrara, A., Kosmas, C., Salvati, L., Padula, A., Mancino, G., & Nolè, A. (2020). Updating the MEDALUS-ESA framework for worldwide land degradation and desertification assessment. *Land Degradation & Development*, *31*(12), 1593–1607.

Francaviglia, R., Di Bene, C., Farina, R., Salvati, L., & Vicente-Vicente, J. L. (2019). Assessing "4 per 1000" soil organic carbon storage rates under Mediterranean climate: A comprehensive data analysis. *Mitigation and Adaptation Strategies for Global Change*, *24*, 795–818.

Gül, E., & Esen, S. (2024). High desertification susceptibility in forest ecosystems revealed by the Environmental Sensitivity Area Index (ESAI). *Sustainability*, *16*(23), 10409. https://doi.org/10.3390/su162310409

Halbac-Cotoara-Zamfir, R., Smiraglia, D., Quaranta, G., Salvia, R., Salvati, L., & Giménez-Morera, A. (2020). Land degradation and mitigation policies in the Mediterranean Region: A brief commentary. *Sustainability*, *12*(20), 8313. https://doi.org/10.3390/su12208313

Imbrenda, V., Coluzzi, R., Di Stefano, V., Egidi, G., Salvati, L., Samela, C., Simoniello, T., & Lanfredi, M. (2022). Modeling spatio-temporal divergence in land vulnerability to desertification with local regressions. *Sustainability*, *14*(17), 10906. https://doi.org/10.3390/su141710906

Imbrenda, V., Gómez, C. M., D'Emilio, M., Samela, C., Salvati, L., Matarazzo, N., Lanfredi, M., & Coluzzi, R. (2023). Remote sensing and spatial databases for investigating latent urban-rural dynamics in rural, inland districts of Southern Italy. *Cuadernos de Investigación Geográfica: Geographical Research Letters*, *49*(2), 143–162. https://doi.org/10.18172/cig.5806

Imbrenda, V., Maialetti, M., Sateriano, A., Scarpitta, D., Quaranta, G., Chelli, F., & Salvati, L. (2024). Scrutinizing the statistical distribution of a composite index of soil degradation as a measure of early desertification risk in advanced economies. *Environments*, *11*(11), 246. https://doi.org/10.3390/environments11110246

Incerti, G., Feoli, E., Salvati, L., Brunetti, A., & Giovacchini, A. (2007). Analysis of bioclimatic time series and their neural network-based classification to characterise drought risk patterns in South Italy. *International Journal of Biometeorology*, *51*, 253–263.

Jakubínský, J., Prokopová, M., Raška, P., Salvati, L., Bezak, N., Cudlín, O., Cudlín, P., Purkyt, J., Vezza, P., Camporeale, C., Daněk, J., Pástor, M., & Lepeška, T. (2021). Managing floodplains using nature-based solutions to support multiple ecosystem functions and services. *Wiley Interdisciplinary Reviews: Water*, *8*(5), e1545.

Kairis, O., Kosmas, C., Karavitis, C., Ritsema, C., Salvati, L., Acikalin, S., Alcalá, M., Alfama, P., Atlhopheng, J., Barrera, J., Belgacem, A., Solé-Benet, A., Brito, J., Chaker, M., Chanda, R., Coelho, C., Darkoh, M., Diamantis, I., Ermolaeva, O., … Ziogas, A. (2014). Evaluation and selection of indicators for land degradation and desertification monitoring: Types of degradation, causes, and implications for management. *Environmental Management*, *54*, 971–982.

Kosmas, C., Kairis, O., Karavitis, C., Acikalin, S., Alcalá, M., Alfama, P., Atlhopheng, J., Barrera, J., Belgacem, A., Solé-Benet, A., Brito, J., Chaker, M., Chanda, R., Darkoh, M., Ermolaeva, O., Fassouli, V., Fernandez, F., Gokceoglu, C., Gonzalez, D., Gungor, H., … Salvati, L. (2015). An exploratory analysis of land abandonment drivers in areas prone to desertification. *Catena*, *128*, 252–261.

Mancino, G., Nolè, A., Salvati, L., & Ferrara, A. (2016). In-between forest expansion and cropland decline: A revised USLE model for soil erosion risk under land-use change in a Mediterranean region. *Ecological Indicators*, *71*, 544–550.

Matarazzo, N., Coluzzi, R., Imbrenda, V., Lanfredi, M., Galella, M., & Krauss, D. R. (2025). The role of peripherality in the spread of pandemic: Evidence from Basilicata (Southern Italy) during the first wave of COVID-19. *International Journal of Disaster Risk Reduction*, *122*, 105457. https://doi.org/10.1016/j.ijdrr.2025.105457

Metternicht, G., Akhtar-Schuster, M., & Castillo, V. (2019). Implementing land degradation neutrality: From policy challenges to policy opportunities for national sustainable development. *Environmental Science & Policy*, *100*, 189–191. https://doi.org/10.1016/j.envsci.2019.07.010

Morin, E. (1973). *Le Paradigme perdu – La nature humaine*, Le Seuil, Paris.

Pace, L., Imbrenda, V., Lanfredi, M., Cudlín, P., Simoniello, T., Salvati, L., & Coluzzi, R. (2023). Delineating the intrinsic, long-term path of land degradation: A spatially explicit transition matrix for Italy, 1960–2010. *International Journal of Environmental Research and Public Health*, *20*(3), 2402. https://doi.org/10.3390/ijerph20032402

Pani, P. (2020). *Land degradation and socio-economic development: A field-based perspective*. Springer International Publishing. https://doi.org/10.1007/978-3-030-42074-1

Perini, L., Salvati, L., Ceccarelli, T., Motisi, A., Marra, F. P., & Caruso, T. (2007). Atlante agroclimatico – Scenari di cambiamento climatico. CRA-UCEA, Roma, *Collana Climagri n. 52 (Atlante + CD)*, 72 pagine. ISBN 88-901472-8-8.

Quaranta, G., Salvia, R., Salvati, L., Paola, V. D., Coluzzi, R., Imbrenda, V., & Simoniello, T. (2020). Long-term impacts of grazing management on land degradation in a rural community of Southern Italy: Depopulation matters. *Land Degradation & Development*, *31*(16), 2379–2394.

Ragosta, M., Daniele, G., Imbrenda, V., Coluzzi, R., D'Emilio, M., Lanfredi, M., & Matarazzo, N. (2024). Land transformations in Irpinia (Southern Italy): A tale on the socio-economic dynamics acting in a marginal area of the Mediterranean Europe. *Sustainability*, *16*(19), 8724. https://doi.org/10.3390/su16198724

Rajbanshi, J., & Das, S. (2021). Monitoring land sensitivity to desertification using the ESAI approach and evaluation of the key indicators: A spatio-temporal study in India. *Land Degradation & Development*, *32*(10), 3045–3061. https://doi.org/10.1002/ldr.3965

Sallustio, L., Pettenella, D., Merlini, P., Romano, R., Salvati, L., Marchetti, M., & Corona, P. (2018). Assessing the economic marginality of agricultural lands in Italy to support land use planning. *Land Use Policy*, *76*, 526–534.

Salvati, L. (2013). Monitoring high-quality soil consumption driven by urban pressure in a growing city (Rome, Italy). *Cities*, *31*, 349–356.

Salvati, L., & Bajocco, S. (2011). Land sensitivity to desertification across Italy: Past, present, and future. *Applied Geography*, *31*(1), 223–231. https://doi.org/10.1016/j.apgeog.2010.04.006

Salvati, L., Bajocco, S., Ceccarelli, T., Zitti, M., & Perini, L. (2011). Towards a process-based evaluation of land vulnerability to soil degradation in Italy. *Ecological Indicators*, *11*(5), 1216–1227.

Salvati, L., & Carlucci, M. (2014). A composite index of sustainable development at the local scale: Italy as a case study. *Ecological Indicators*, *43*, 162–171.

Salvati, L., Mavrakis, A., Colantoni, A., Mancino, G., & Ferrara, A. (2015). Complex Adaptive Systems, soil degradation and land sensitivity to desertification: A multivariate assessment of Italian agro-forest landscape. *Science of the Total Environment*, *521*, 235–245.

Salvati, L., Perini, L., Sabbi, A., & Bajocco, S. (2012). Climate aridity and land use changes: A regional-scale analysis. *Geographical Research*, *50*(2), 193–203.

Salvati, L., & Zitti, M. (2005). Land degradation in the Mediterranean basin: Linking bio-physical and economic factors into an ecological perspective. *Biota*, *6*, 67–77.

Salvati, L., & Zitti, M. (2008). Regional convergence of environmental variables: Empirical evidences from land degradation. *Ecological Economics*, *68*(1–2), 162–168.

Salvati, L., & Zitti, M. (2009). Substitutability and weighting of ecological and economic indicators: Exploring the importance of various components of a synthetic index. *Ecological Economics*, *68*(4), 1093–1099.

Salvati, L., Zitti, M., & Ceccarelli, T. (2008). Integrating economic and environmental indicators in the assessment of desertification risk: A case study. *Applied Ecological and Environmental Research*, *6*(1), 129–138.

Salvati, L., Zitti, M., Ceccarelli, T., & Perini, L. (2009). Developing a synthetic index of land vulnerability to drought and desertification. *Geographical Research*, *47*(3), 280–291. https://doi.org/10.1111/j.1745-5871.2009.00590.x

Seifollahi-Aghmiuni, S., Kalantari, Z., Egidi, G., Gaburova, L., & Salvati, L. (2022). Urbanisation-driven land degradation and socioeconomic challenges in peri-urban areas: Insights from Southern Europe. *Ambio*, *51*(6), 1446–1458.

Sklenicka, P., Zouhar, J., Molnarova, K. J., Vlasak, J., Kottova, B., Petrzelka, P., Gebhart, M., & Walmsley, A. (2020). Trends of soil degradation: Does the socio-economic status of land owners and land users matter? *Land Use Policy*, *95*, 103992. https://doi.org/10.1016/j.landusepol.2019.05.011

Tomao, A., Quatrini, V., Corona, P., Ferrara, A., Lafortezza, R., & Salvati, L. (2017). Resilient landscapes in Mediterranean urban areas: Understanding factors influencing forest trends. *Environmental Research*, *156*, 1–9.

Wilson, G. A., & Juntti, M. (2005). *Unravelling desertification: Policies and actor networks in Southern Europe*. Wageningen Acad. Publ. https://doi.org/10.3920/978-90-8686-559-8

Wilson, G. A., Kelly, C. L., Briassoulis, H., Ferrara, A., Quaranta, G., Salvia, R., Detsis, V., Curfs, M., Cerda, A., El-Aich, A., Liu, H., Kosmas, C., Alados, C. L., Imeson, A., Landgrebe-Trinkunaite, R., Salvati, L., Naumann, S., Danwen, H., Iosifides, T., … Zhang, P. (2017). Social memory and the resilience of communities affected by land degradation. *Land Degradation & Development*, *28*(2), 383–400.

6

SEEKING OPTIMAL WASTE MANAGEMENT IN ADVANCED ECONOMIES

CLIO CIASCHINI[a], MARCO MAIALETTI[b], DONATO SCARPITTA[c], ADELE SATERIANO[d], LUCA SALVATI[e], YURI CORRADI[f], MAURIZIO MASI[g] AND LUIGI FICI[g]

[a]*Polytechnic University of Marche, Italy*
[b]*Independent Researcher and Lawyer, Rome, Italy*
[c]*Independent Research and Architect, Salerno, Italy*
[d]*Mediterranean Sustainable Development Foundation (MEDES), Italy*
[e]*Sapienza University of Rome, Italy*
[f]*Italian National Statistical Institute, Italy*
[g]*Tuscia University, Italy*

ABSTRACT

Waste management is a key issue in regional science and sustainable development, particularly characterising rural areas. The study of this issue should be coupled with a proper evaluation of the subjective perspective of households and families – representing the main territorial actors along with businesses and institutions. This chapter therefore analyses the behaviours of Italian families on separate waste collection and their perception of some issues of this complex environmental problem, such as the accessibility to differentiated waste collection bins, with a specific focus on rural areas. This issue – addressing societal concerns – should conclude the interpretative circle, from economics to society, passing through the environmental topics covered in the central chapters of this book.

Keywords: Perception; household; survey; official statistics; Italy

INTRODUCTION

Waste management represents a fundamental challenge in the areas of regional science and sustainable development (Mihai et al., 2021). A proper waste management contributes to reducing environmental pollution, preserving natural resources and improving the quality of life of individuals and the social cohesion in local communities. In line with the Sustainable Development Goals (SDGs) of the United Nations, especially Goal 11 (Cities and sustainable communities) and Goal 12 (Responsible production and consumption), effective waste management is crucial to promote more eco-compatible practices (Elsheekh et al., 2021). Differentiated collection strategies, reuse, and recycling are key instruments to lower the environmental footprint and favour a more sustainable development model (Abubakar et al., 2022; Pujara et al., 2019; Srivastav & Kumar, 2021). Within this context, this chapter investigates quantitatively the behaviours and perceptions of Italian families on differentiated waste quantitatively, focusing specifically on urban collection of solid waste and the related evaluation of road dirtiness of neighbourhoods, as a consequence of partly ineffective waste collection (Sharma et al., 2021). The necessary data and information, with specific reference to Italy, have been retrieved from official statistics – more specifically from the multi-scope survey on income and life conditions of residents carried out with homogeneous criteria at the European level.

Even with still relevant territorial imbalances between northern economically dynamic regions and southern disadvantaged regions, Italy was experiencing – especially in a relatively short time period associated with moderate economic expansion before the huge stagnation following the 2008 global financial crisis – a rapid transition from traditional models of waste management to more advanced and technologically significant strategies of waste disposal and valorisation. By specifically investigating such a time period, the present work assumes such transitions as a consequence of a long period of socio-environmental crisis in the 1990s and the early 2000s – with the management of solid urban waste as an element of environmental depletion connected with a constant and pervasive economic development (Dijkema et al., 2000).

More specifically, this period lays the foundations for the subsequent waste management in line with more advanced and innovative logics (Gaeta et al., 2021). Significant evolutions in the perception of families have, somehow, led these transformations to the present context, within a context of economic and environmental crisis, but also of increasing social sensibilisation towards topics of sustainability and safeguard of the environment (Cheah et al., 2022). Among other countries, Italy is going through a renewal process, despite the several territorial disparities between the more dynamic and industrialised northern regions, and the southern regions, still lagging in the implementation of the policies of waste management (Mazzanti et al., 2008).

In some northern areas, systems of differentiated collection of waste have resulted in being more efficient, and an increasing attention has been given to waste reduction, while in Southern Italy, many cultural, infrastructural and logistic obstacles have been reported (Agovino et al., 2017; De Rosa, 2018; Salvati et al., 2013). As explained before, the analysed period mainly extends before the global financial crisis of 2008–2009, an historical moment in which the management system of waste was still in a phase of consolidation and development of more sustainable strategies (Lakhouit, 2025). In this phase, the basis for a new management model has been traced, which should then have found full development in the subsequent decades (Barr et al., 2011). The economic crisis, indeed, highly affects the number of resources devoted to waste management, inducing local and national administrations to review their own strategies and adopt more efficient solutions, also introducing innovative technologies and incentives to differentiated collection (Sharma et al., 2020).

The core of this study relates to the perception of Italian families on the differentiated collection and to the environmental conditions of their own territory (Carlucci et al., 2022; Salvati & Carlucci, 2014). A special focus has been put on the accessibility to differentiated collection containers and the presence of dirt on urban roads, directly affecting the life quality and the environmental awareness of citizens. The perceptions, indeed, are not only the result of objective information, but they are deeply affected by cultural, social and territorial factors, thus representing a key element to understand the dynamics of adhesion to sustainability practices (Obirih-Opareh & Post, 2002). The work relies on the data retrieved from official statistics, providing a detailed picture of habits and opinions of Italian families with reference to waste management and the care of the urban environment. More specifically, data from the 'survey on lifestyle and consumption of families' (EUSILC) have also been considered, an informative European panel updated yearly, allowing to compare Italian dynamics with those of other European countries.

This comparative approach allows to highlight similarities and differences in the individual perceptions and behaviours, thus offering a more articulated and complete framework of current transformations (Jaeger-Erben et al., 2015). The research highlights the temporal evolution of opinions and perceptions of Italian families in response to different occurrences, among which are the sensibilisation campaigns, technological innovations and public policies (Shevchenko et al., 2019). In addition, these transformations supported the creation of a more favourable context to the spread of truly effective and sustainable practices of differentiated waste collection (Fig. 6.1), even with still persisting challenges, particularly connected to territorial disparities and cultural resistance (Seifollahi-Aghmiuni et al., 2022). In general, our study provides a global vision of social and environmental dynamics characterising the interaction between Italian families and waste management practices (Castellano et al., 2019; McCormick et al., 2013; Pierini et al., 2021). The subjective approach, supported by official statistical data, allows to identify the peculiarities of perceptions to better understand the motivations behind more sustainable behaviours, to face the future challenges and build an always greener and aware landscape (Fiorillo & Senatore, 2020).

Fig. 6.1 Urban Settlements as Laboratory of Creative and Innovative Practices of Waste Collection and Management.
Source: Authors' Photographic Archive.

EMPIRICAL FINDINGS

In 2006, nearly 6 out of 10 families declare of always doing the differentiated waste collection of paper, 60% of glass, 46% of drugs, 43% of cans and aluminium, 54% of plastic containers, 50% of organic waste, and 23% of other typologies of waste, among which wood and bulky waste (Table 6.1). The increase in waste collection participation over time was rather evident. Considering, on average, all typologies of waste, this increase equals about five percentage points, with even higher percentages for paper, aluminium, plastic food containers, and organic waste.

In Northern Italy, more than 80% of families declared to do the differentiated waste of paper, and more than 60% of them routinely collected other typologies of waste differently – except for the category labelled as 'other', for which 34% and 41% of families have been registered respectively in North-Western and North-Eastern regions. These percentages decreased in Southern Italy; specifically, 9% to 30% for organic wastes in the major Italian islands, Sicily and Sardinia (Table 6.2). A more disaggregated geographic analysis, at the regional level or by district profiles, remarks the existing territorial disparities already mentioned above (Table 6.3).

Considering the percentage of families doing a differentiated collection of several typologies of waste (47% at national level), relevant differences have been observed between Northern regions (largely over the share of 50%, with the only relevant exception of Liguria) and Southern regions (all constantly below 40% with sometimes negligible values, as those registered in Calabria and Sicily, except for – even slight – recovery observed in Sardinia). In conclusion, data analysis by typology of municipality shows that, for all typology of waste – except for plastic food containers – the percentage of families declaring differentiated waste collection is elevated in municipalities with populations ranging from 2,000 to 10,000 inhabitants. Lower percentages were often related to major municipalities (over 50,000 inhabitants and those located in the centre of a metropolitan area). Compared with previous years, increases have been registered across all typologies of waste collection. Higher increases have been reported for families declaring to do a systematic, differentiated collection of used batteries, aluminium cans, drugs and organic waste.

Data on the accessibility to containers highlight some differences connected with the typology of waste (Table 6.4). On average, only 58% of the interviewed families declare that the containers are easily accessible in their neighbourhood. Specifically, these percentages vary from 57% for glass and paper, to 29% and 36% respectively for used batteries and drugs. The share

Table 6.1 Per Cent Share of Families Doing Differentiated Waste Collection.

Year	Differentiated Collection of Waste															
	Paper		Glass		Drugs		Used batteries		Aluminium cans		Plastic food containers		Organic waste		Other[a]	
	Always	Sometimes	Always	Sometimes	Always	Sometimes	Always	Sometimes	Always	Sometimes	Always	Sometimes	Always	Sometimes	Always	Sometimes
2000	51.5	16.6	56.5	16.4	39.7	17.4	36.2	15.5	32.5	13.6	45.3	13.7	41.4	7.3	14.4	5.3
2001	52.5	17.2	56.2	17.3	39.6	17.5	36.5	15.4	34.3	14.5	46.8	14.2	44.7	7.9	15.8	5.3
2002	54.4	16.2	57	16.3	41.5	16.5	38	14.9	36.9	13	48	13.3	45.7	7.7	22	6.7
2003	55.2	16.1	57.3	16.6	40.5	16.7	37.3	15.1	37.5	14.1	49.5	14.2	46.3	8.5	21.4	7.1
2005	56.5	15.5	59.6	14.8	43	16	39.2	14.8	40.2	12.7	52.1	12.4	47.4	7.8	20.8	5.3
2006	58.6	14.6	60.4	14.6	45.8	14.7	42.8	12.8	43.2	11.8	53.8	12.2	50.5	7.7	23.2	5.5

Source: EUSILC, Istat/Eurostat.

[a]The option 'other' includes containers for the differentiated collection of materials, such as woods, syringes, ferrous materials, bulky waste, and lead accumulators.

Table 6.2. Per Cent Share of Families Applying Differentiated Waste Collection by Geographical Area.

	Differentiated Collection of Waste															
Year	**Paper**		**Glass**		**Drugs**		**Used batteries**		**Aluminium cans**		**Plastic food containers**		**Organic waste**		**Other[a]**	
	Always	**Sometimes**	**Always**	**Sometimes**	**Always**	**Sometimes**	**Always**	**Sometimes**	**Always**	**Sometimes**	**Always**	**Sometimes**	**Always**	**Sometimes**	**Always**	**Sometimes**
Italy	**58.6**	**14.6**	**60.4**	**14.6**	**45.8**	**14.7**	**42.8**	**12.8**	**43.2**	**11.8**	**53.8**	**12.2**	**50.5**	**7.7**	**23.2**	**5.5**
North-west	81.8	8.4	84.2	8.1	63.2	13.3	60.3	12.1	62.5	8.7	76.7	7.7	68.4	6.4	34.2	4.4
North-East	80.4	9.1	80.8	8.2	68.6	9.8	68.2	9.1	67.4	7.9	75.2	7.2	67.1	5.8	42.6	3.7
Centre	49.4	19.8	52	18.8	34.7	17.8	31.7	15.6	33.2	14.8	42.9	15.8	38.1	10.5	11.3	6.4
South	34.7	21.7	35.3	22.8	26	17.7	21.2	14.5	20.4	16	30.3	18.2	33.8	8.3	9.6	8.2
Islands	24.2	16.7	28	18.7	19.5	15	15.5	12.4	14	12.5	23.4	14.7	30.6	8	8.9	4.9

Source: EUSILC, Istat/Eurostat.

[a]The option 'other' includes containers for the differentiated collection of materials, such as woods, syringes, ferrous materials, bulky waste, and lead accumulators.

Table 6.3 Per Cent Share of Families Doing Differentiated Collection of Waste by Municipal Type.

	Differentiated Collection of Waste															
Year	Paper		Glass		Drugs		Used batteries		Aluminium cans		Plastic food containers		Organic waste		Other[a]	
	Always	Sometimes	Always	Sometimes	Always	Sometimes	Always	Sometimes	Always	Sometimes	Always	Sometimes	Always	Sometimes	Always	Sometimes
Municipality centre of the metropolitan area	54	18	54	19	37	18	32	14	36	14	47	15	41	10	12	5
Periphery of the metropolitan area	61	13	62	13	50	13	46	12	51	10	62	10	57	6	27	4
Municipalities up to 2,000 inhabitants	61	12	65	12	50	11	50	10	40	10	50	10	41	7	24	6
Municipalities between 2,001 and 10,000 inhabitants	65	12	68	11	54	13	52	12	52	10	61	10	58	6	31	6

Municipalities between 10,001 and 50,000 inhabitants	57	15	59	15	46	15	44	13	44	11	54	12	54	8	26	6
Municipalities with over 50,000 inhabitants	54	18	55	17	38	16	34	15	34	14	47	16	44	9	16	6

Source: EUSILC, Istat/Eurostat.

[a]The option 'other' includes containers for the differentiated collection of materials, such as woods, syringes, ferrous materials, bulky waste, and lead accumulators.

Table 6.4 Per Cent Share of Families by Degree of Accessibility to Containers for Differentiated Collection of Waste in Their Living Area.

Year	Differentiated Collection of Waste															
	Paper		Glass		Drugs		Used batteries		Aluminium cans		Plastic food containers		Organic waste		Other[a]	
	Easily	Hardly	Easily	Hardly	Easily	Hardly	Easily	Hardly	Easily	Hardly	Easily	Hardly	Easily	Hardly	Easily	Hardly
2000	51	15	56	16	33	18	27	17	32	13	43	14	39	8	11	5
2001	52	15	57	17	33	18	26	17	32	13	43	14	42	8	11	5
2002	55	14	58	16	34	18	28	16	35	13	45	13	45	8	17	5
2003	54	14	57	16	32	18	26	17	35	13	46	13	44	8	16	5
2005	57	12	59	14	35	17	28	16	37	11	48	12	46	7	16	5
2006	57	13	58	15	36	17	29	16	38	12	48	12	47	8	18	5

Source: EUSILC, Istat/Eurostat.

[a]The option 'other' includes containers for the differentiated collection of materials such as woods, syringes, ferrous materials, bulky waste, and lead accumulators.

of residents declaring it too inconvenient to reach the bins for differentiated collection is, on average, around 15%, independently of the typology of waste, with slightly higher percentages when talking about containers for drugs and used batteries.

Compared with the situation recorded in 2005, the share of families declaring easy accessibility to the containers for other typologies of waste (e.g. wood, bulk materials) increases by 8.7%, for organic waste by 3.5%, for used batteries and aluminium cans by 2.9%, for drugs by 2.3%, and by less than 1% for paper and plastic containers. For glass, a slight decrease has been recorded. Data related to macro-geographic areas show the percentages of families able to access containers for each typology of waste (Table 6.5).

Regional data on accessibility of containers for differentiated waste further support the idea of a country running on two speeds, with a northern part placing over the national average, and a southern part resting on rather negligible percentages, especially Campania, Calabria, and Sicily. Central Italy represents, even in this case, the average point between the two spatial trends. Different from the previously analysed phenomena, the classification by typology of municipality does not identify significant differences between small and big municipalities (Table 6.6). Only for paper, an easily differentiated material, the evaluation of the accessibility of containers between urban/metropolitan areas and rural municipalities reports a gap of more than 15 percentage points.

Taken together, this context seems to reflect the deep socioeconomic and cultural differences between the different areas of the country, reflected in huge disparities even in the awareness levels of environmental responsibility. In this perspective, empirical data highlight that, despite a general improvement, in densely populated areas characterised by higher urbanisation, the issue of dirty streets is largely perceived, probably due to the higher flows of traffic, wider quantities of abandoned waste and the supposed difficulty of management of urban garbage collection.

Dirty Roads in Urban Settlements

In 2006, 35% of Italian families raised the issue of dirty roads in their living area (Table 6.7). Throughout the years, starting from 2001, the registered percentage increased by around one percentage point. This trend was clearly observed in all Italian regions, even with different dynamics, partly connected to the different demographic structures and population density. The most affected regions include Latium (53% in 2006, showing a rise of around six

Table 6.5 Per Cent Share of Families by Degree of Accessibility to Containers for Differentiated Collection of Waste Within Their Living Zone by Geographical Area.

	Accessible Recycling Bins for:															
	Paper		Glass		Drugs		Used batteries		Aluminium cans		Plastic food containers		Organic waste		Other[a]	
	Easily	Hardly	Easily	Hardly	Easily	Hardly	Easily	Hardly	Easily	Hardly	Easily	Hardly	Easily	Hardly	Easily	Hardly
Italy	**57**	**13**	**58**	**15**	**36**	**17**	**29**	**16**	**38**	**12**	**48**	**12**	**47**	**8**	**18**	**5**
North-West	68	10	72	12	46	17	39	17	48	9	60	10	57	6	23	5
North-East	70	13	70	15	48	20	45	19	57	13	63	13	59	8	31	5
Centre	60	15	61	15	31	18	24	17	38	14	49	13	45	9	12	4
South	41	16	42	19	23	16	15	14	21	13	32	14	34	9	8	5
Islands	30	12	33	13	19	13	12	10	16	7	24	11	31	7	8	3

Source: EUSILC, Istat/Eurostat.

[a]The option 'other' includes containers for the differentiated collection of materials, such as woods, syringes, ferrous materials, bulky waste, and lead accumulators.

Table 6.6 Per Cent Share of Families by Degree of Accessibility to Containers for Differentiated Collection of Waste in Their Living Area by Typology of Municipality.

	Accessible Recycling Bins for:															
Year	**Paper**		**Glass**		**Drugs**		**Used batteries**		**Aluminium cans**		**Plastic food containers**		**Organic waste**		**Other[a]**	
	Easily	**Hardly**	**Easily**	**Hardly**	**Easily**	**Hardly**	**Easily**	**Hardly**	**Easily**	**Hardly**	**Easily**	**Hardly**	**Easily**	**Hardly**	**Easily**	**Hardly**
Municipality centre of the metropolitan area	67	12	65	15	38	15	23	14	42	11	56	12	49	6	12	4
Periphery of the metropolitan area	58	11	58	11	38	15	30	15	44	8	54	10	50	6	21	3
Municipalities up to 2,000 inhabitants	58	11	62	12	39	16	38	16	36	9	43	9	35	6	19	4
Municipalities between 2,001 and 10,000 inhabitants	51	12	55	15	37	18	35	16	37	11	44	12	45	7	21	5
Municipalities between 10,001 and 50,000 inhabitants	52	14	55	15	31	20	26	18	35	14	45	14	48	9	18	7
Municipalities with over 50,000 inhabitants	60	15	61	16	35	15	26	15	38	13	51	14	50	10	15	5

Source: EUSILC, Istat/Eurostat.

[a]The option 'other' includes containers for the differentiated collection of materials, such as woods, syringes, ferrous materials, bulky waste, and lead accumulators.

Table 6.7 Per Cent Share of Families Complaining About Dirty Roads in Their Living Area by Administrative Region[a] and Year.

Administrative Region	2001	2002	2003	2005	2006
Piedmont	33.6	33.2	31.3	31.9	37.8
Aosta valley	18.9	13.8	10.8	14.6	19.0
Lombardia	37.0	32.1	32.3	32.5	36.2
Trentino-Alto Adige	15.9	14.9	15.4	18.1	21.2
Veneto	26.9	26.9	24.6	24.3	28.6
Friuli-Venezia Giulia	26.1	26.6	20.7	25.3	24.0
Liguria	41.9	43.6	40.2	40.2	42.8
Emilia-Romagna	26.2	18.6	25.0	20.3	24.3
Tuscany	36.7	29.3	29.7	30.8	29.6
Umbria	21.5	23.9	26.2	27.5	30.9
Marche	20.9	24.2	23.2	25.8	23.8
Latium	47.2	48.2	51.6	49.1	52.9
Abruzzo	21.0	22.0	26.2	29.7	25.5
Molise	22.4	22.8	24.4	27.0	21.9
Campania	38.2	39.4	44.3	47.4	45.5
Apulia	29.1	25.1	26.9	27.4	28.7
Basilicata	29.6	23.5	23.8	23.9	32.8
Calabria	31.7	27.0	31.0	31.9	36.0
Sicily	34.9	29.3	32.0	30.1	33.1
Sardinia	36.4	28.6	29.8	38.5	33.1
Italy	**33.8**	**31.1**	**32.5**	**32.6**	**34.9**

Source: EUSILC, Istat/Eurostat.

[a]Percentage of families declaring the problem as 'much or enough' evident.

percentage points from 2001), Campania (46% in 2006, with an increase by around eight percentage points from 2001) and Liguria (43% in 2006, with an increase by about one percentage point from 2001).

In 2006, the percentage of families declaring the presence of issues related to dirt on roads varies from 26% in Northeast to 40% in Centre (Table 6.8). Anyway, the highest increases are reported in Southern Italy, with an additional average around 4%, while the same percentage remains rather unchanged (slightly diminishing) in northern regions and islands.

Sharper variations have been reported in aggregate data by typology of municipality (Table 6.9). In metropolitan centres, the inconvenience has been perceived by 59% of families, while in small municipalities (up to 2,000 inhabitants) only 21% of families complain about this situation. With respect to 2005, families declaring 'much' or 'enough' evident, perceptions about road

Table 6.8. Per Cent Share of Families Complaining About Dirty Roads in Their Living Area by Geographical Area[a] and Year.

Region	2001	2002	2003	2005	2006
Italy	**33.8**	**31.1**	**32.5**	**32.6**	**34.9**
North-west	36.5	33.6	32.8	33.0	37.3
North-east	25.6	22.6	23.5	22.3	25.8
Centre	38.8	37.4	39.4	38.6	40.1
South	32.2	30.6	34.1	35.9	36.0
Islands	35.3	29.1	31.4	32.1	33.1

Source: Istat, Indagine multiscopo sulle famiglie – Aspetti della vita quotidiana.

[a]Percentage of families declaring the problem as 'much or enough' evident.

Table 6.9. Per Cent Share of Families Complaining About Dirty Roads in Their Living Area by Typology of Municipality[a] and Year.

Municipal Type	2001	2002	2003	2005	2006
Municipal centre of the respective metropolitan area	56.1	54.5	55.8	57.5	59.4
Periphery of the metropolitan area	33.8	30.8	35.6	34.2	38.7
Municipalities up to 2,000 inhabitants	16.4	22.0	16.4	18.6	21.3
Municipalities between 2,001 and 10,000 inhabitants	23.4	19.7	22.9	23.0	24.1
Municipalities between 10,001 and 50,000 inhabitants	31.4	26.6	27.7	26.5	29.7
Municipalities above 50,000 inhabitants	34.8	32.9	33.3	34.1	36.0
Italy	**33.8**	**31.1**	**32.5**	**32.6**	**34.9**

Source: Istat, Indagine multiscopo sulle famiglie – Aspetti della vita quotidiana, different years.

[a]Per cent share of families declaring the problem 'much or enough' present.

dirtiness in their living area increased by more than two percentage points. In absolute terms, wider increases were reported in urban and peri-urban areas (respectively 3% and 5%) and, almost surprisingly, even in municipalities with up to 2,000 inhabitants (5%).

DISCUSSION

The present work provides a detailed – while exploratory – investigation on the participation of the Italian families to differentiated waste collection, the perception of road dirtiness in their living area and, as a possibly related topic, the accessibility to containers for differentiated collection (Egidi et al., 2020). These indicators are crucial to understand the present state of waste management and the still persisting territorial disparities in the study area (e.g. Coluzzi et al., 2022), thus highlighting challenges and opportunities to improve the systems of collection and raise awareness in resident populations (Wekisa & Majale, 2020). At the end of the study period, a relevant increase has been highlighted in the participation of Italian families to the differentiated collection with respect to the past years. On average, 54%–59% of families declare to usually do the differentiated collection of various materials, reporting higher percentages in Northern regions and lower percentages in Southern regions. In some North-Western and North-Eastern regions, more than 80% of families declare to 'always' do the collection of paper and more than 60% of other materials, while in Southern areas these percentages significantly decrease, reaching values of 9%–30% for some typologies as 'other', and bulky waste.

This territorial disparity reflects the structural and economic peculiarities between the different areas of the country (e.g. Salvati & Carlucci, 2011), but also the degree of awareness, and the intimate structure and efficiency in the operational system of waste collection (Vardopoulos et al., 2021). A higher environmental (and civic) awareness, and the spread of effective services in Northern Italy resulted in a higher participation to differentiated waste collection, while in the South, there still are relevant criticalities connected to both cultural factors and infrastructural delays (David Jr et al., 2020). Throughout time, a growing participation, particularly for differential collection of specific materials such as used batteries, aluminium cans, organic waste and drugs, indicates an increasing environmental awareness and a possible improvement of the recycling practices (Nandy et al., 2022). This suggests that, despite huge territorial disparities, environmental education seems to be effective (Mmereki et al., 2016).

The accessibility to containers for differentiated waste collection represents another relevant element of analysis, since it directly affects the participation of families to best practices (Ahmed & Ali, 2004; Cheng & Mao, 2024; Joseph, 2006). In 2006, around 58% of families declared that the containers are easily accessible, although with significant territorial differences. North-Western and North-Eastern areas exhibit the highest percentages (more than 68%–70%), while the islands and Some southern areas present much lower values (around 30%–40%). Differences between macro-geographic areas also emerge in the analysis by municipal type. Urban and peri-urban areas, and especially metropolitan centres, report higher percentages of accessibility with respect to rural areas, even if these latter highlight some improvements with respect to the past (Appleyard & Lintell, 1972). The difficulty to access containers, more accentuated in Southern districts and rural areas, hinders the potential increase in public participation, further sharpening the gap between northern and southern areas (Mutatkar, 1995).

Generally speaking, data highlight an easier accessibility to containers for materials as paper and glass with respect to those for drugs or used batteries (Boiral, 2009; Chioatto & Sospiro, 2023; Wilson et al., 2012). An increasing perception of inaccessibility, even representing a minority, could anyway discourage families to properly do the differentiated collection, thereby addressing the missing optimisation of the system (e.g. Nkwachukwu et al., 2010), and possibly influencing related aspects, such as road cleanness (Velis et al., 2012). Between 2005 and 2006, the progressively increasing proportion of families complaining about this issue, in particular in urban and metropolitan areas, should be interpreted as a signal of deteriorating conditions in urban environments (De Feo & De Gisi, 2010), possibly affecting life quality and the motivation of citizens to participate to initiatives of differentiated waste collection (Brotosusilo et al., 2022; Hawkins & Wang, 2012; Marello & Helwege, 2018).

Nevertheless, strong territorial and infrastructural disparities still persist, requiring interventions that promote a more uniform and effective system over the whole national territory (D'Adamo et al., 2022; Garcés et al., 2002; Guerrero et al., 2013). Future policies should aim at strengthening the spatial distribution of collection services, improving the accessibility to containers, and incentivising campaigns of cultural sensibilisation particularly in southern areas and rural zones (Budica et al., 2015; Mazzanti & Zoboli, 2008; Tansel, 2017). Only through a shared commitment between institutions, citizens and operators of the sector, a proper level of environmental sustainability could be reached for present and future challenges (Agrawal & Lemos, 2007). The lack of proper infrastructures, resources and initiatives of environmental education in the most disadvantaged areas represents significant obstacles to be faced with specific policies and a wide involvement of local communities (Iyamu et al., 2022; Marshall & Farahbakhsh, 2013; Subri et al., 2025).

A further element of criticality relates to the issue of dirtiness and urban *décor*, perceived as very present particularly in densely populated areas and big cities (Awino & Apitz, 2024; Okeke et al., 2024; Puvača et al., 2025). The presence of abandoned waste not only affects negatively life quality of citizens, but it can also reduce the motivation to participate to practices of differentiated collection (Agovino et al., 2023; Owusu, 2010; Romano et al., 2022). Future perspectives should delineate a multilevel and integrated strategy to improve the process of waste management (Wolsink, 2010).

It is crucial to implement and reinforce further collection services, ensuring a capillary and uniform accessibility even in the less developed areas (Baud et al., 2001; Ferronato et al., 2019; Hornsby et al., 2017). The formation and environmental education should be empowered, involving schools, communities and local associations to develop a social culture of sustainability (Diduck, 1999; Garofalo et al., 2019; Yasmeen et al., 2023). Moreover, the technological innovation can represent a key element optimising the modalities of collection, management and valorisation of waste, thus supporting a more efficient and less environmentally impacting model (Prata et al., 2025). Similarly to other countries, Italy faces the challenge of combining economic development and environmental safeguard, and is increasingly requested to adopt a sustainable, inclusive model of waste management capable to reduce territorial disparities (Læssoe, 2010; Musella et al., 2019; Singh et al., 2024).

CONCLUDING REMARKS

Improvements towards a sustainable waste management constitute an opportunity to promote a more responsible development model respecting the environment and can be attained only through a commitment shared between the institutions, citizens and operators of the sector. As observed in the case study, the slow path of improvement started at the beginning of the investigated time interval represents a solid basis on which to build future, more effective strategies. The awareness of citizens, quality of infrastructures and social cohesion will be determinant to overcome still existing criticalities, thus achieving a long-term effective and sustainable balanced system of waste management. In this way, Italy – and more generally Mediterranean countries – could face present and future environmental challenges, thus contributing to a cleaner world respectful of natural resources.

REFERENCES

Abubakar, I. R., Maniruzzaman, K. M., Dano, U. L., AlShihri, F. S., AlShammari, M. S., Ahmed, S. M. S., & Alrawaf, T. I. (2022). Environmental sustainability impacts of solid waste management practices in the global South. *International Journal of Environmental Research and Public Health*, *19*(19), 12717.

Agovino, M., Casaccia, M., & Crociata, A. (2017). Effectiveness and efficiency of European Regional Development Fund on separate waste collection: Evidence from Italian regions by a stochastic frontier approach. *Economia Politica*, *34*(1), 105–137.

Agovino, M., Cerciello, M., Javed, A., & Rapposelli, A. (2023). Environmental legislation and waste management efficiency in Italian regions in view of circular economy goals. *Utilities Policy*, *85*, 101675.

Agrawal, A., & Lemos, M. C. (2007). A greener revolution in the making? Environmental governance in the 21st century. *Environment: Science and Policy for Sustainable Development*, *49*(5), 36–45.

Ahmed, S. A., & Ali, M. (2004). Partnerships for solid waste management in developing countries: linking theories to realities. *Habitat international*, *28*(3), 467–479.

Appleyard, D., & Lintell, M. (1972). The environmental quality of city streets: The residents' viewpoint. *Journal of the American Institute of Planners*, *38*(2), 84–101.

Awino, F. B., & Apitz, S. E. (2024). Solid waste management in the context of the waste hierarchy and circular economy frameworks: An international critical review. *Integrated Environmental Assessment and Management*, *20*(1), 9–35.

Barr, S., Gilg, A., & Shaw, G. (2011). Citizens, consumers and sustainability: (Re) Framing environmental practice in an age of climate change. *Global Environmental Change*, *21*(4), 1224–1233.

Baud, I. S. A., Grafakos, S., Hordijk, M., & Post, J. (2001). Quality of life and alliances in solid waste management: Contributions to urban sustainable development. *Cities*, *18*(1), 3–12.

Boiral, O. (2009). Greening the corporation through organizational citizenship behaviors. *Journal of Business Ethics*, *87*(2), 221–236.

Brotosusilo, A., Utari, D., Negoro, H. A., Firdaus, A., & Velentina, R. A. (2022). Community empowerment of waste management in the urban environment: More attention on waste issues through formal and informal educations. *Global Journal of Environmental Science and Management, 8*(2), 209–224.

Budica, I., Busu, O. V., Dumitru, A., & Purcaru, M. L. (2015). Waste management as commitment and duty of citizens. *Polish Journal of Management Studies, 11*(1), 7–16.

Carlucci, M., Salvia, R., Quaranta, G., Salvati, L., & Imbrenda, V. (2022). Official statistics, spatio-temporal dynamics and local-scale monitoring: Toward integrated environmental-economic accounting for land degradation. *Letters in Spatial and Resource Sciences, 15*(3), 469–491.

Castellano, R., Musella, G., & Punzo, G. (2019). The effect of environmental attitudes and policies on separate waste collection: The case of Insular Italy. *Letters in Spatial and Resource Sciences, 12*(1), 63–85.

Cheah, C. G., Chia, W. Y., Lai, S. F., Chew, K. W., Chia, S. R., & Show, P. L. (2022). Innovation designs of industry 4.0 based solid waste management: Machinery and digital circular economy. *Environmental Research, 213*, 113619.

Cheng, H., & Mao, C. (2024). Disparities in environmental behavior from urban–rural perspectives: how socioeconomic status structures influence residents' environmental actions—based on the 2021 China general social survey data. *Sustainability, 16*(18), 7886.

Chioatto, E., & Sospiro, P. (2023). Transition from waste management to circular economy: The European Union roadmap. *Environment, Development and Sustainability, 25*(1), 249–276.

Coluzzi, R., Bianchini, L., Egidi, G., Cudlin, P., Imbrenda, V., Salvati, L., & Lanfredi, M. (2022). Density matters? Settlement expansion and land degradation in peri-urban and rural districts of Italy. *Environmental Impact Assessment Review, 92*, 106703.

D'Adamo, I., Mazzanti, M., Morone, P., & Rosa, P. (2022). Assessing the relation between waste management policies and circular economy goals. *Waste Management, 154*, 27–35.

David Jr, V. E., John, Y., & Hussain, S. (2020). Rethinking sustainability: A review of Liberia's municipal solid waste management systems, status, and challenges. *Journal of Material Cycles and Waste Management, 22*(5), 1299–1317.

De Feo, G., & De Gisi, S. (2010). Public opinion and awareness towards MSW and separate collection programmes: A sociological procedure for selecting areas and citizens with a low level of knowledge. *Waste Management, 30*(6), 958–976.

De Rosa, S. P. (2018). A political geography of 'waste wars' in Campania (Italy): Competing territorialisations and socio-environmental conflicts. *Political Geography, 67*, 46–55.

Diduck, A. (1999). Critical education in resource and environmental management: Learning and empowerment for a sustainable future. *Journal of Environmental Management, 57*(2), 85–97.

Dijkema, G. P. J., Reuter, M. A., & Verhoef, E. V. (2000). A new paradigm for waste management. *Waste Management, 20*(8), 633–638.

Egidi, G., Salvati, L., & Vinci, S. (2020). The long way to tipperary: City size and worldwide urban population trends, 1950–2030. *Sustainable Cities and Society, 60*, 102148.

Elsheekh, K. M., Kamel, R. R., Elsherif, D. M., & Shalaby, A. M. (2021). Achieving sustainable development goals from the perspective of solid waste management plans. *Journal of Engineering and Applied Science, 68*(1), 9.

Ferronato, N., Rada, E. C., Portillo, M. A. G., Cioca, L. I., Ragazzi, M., & Torretta, V. (2019). Introduction of the circular economy within developing regions: A comparative analysis of advantages and opportunities for waste valorization. *Journal of Environmental Management, 230*, 366–378.

Fiorillo, D., & Senatore, L. (2020). Pro-social behaviours, waste concern and recycling behaviour in Italy at the end of the 1990s. *Environmental Economics and Policy Studies, 22*(2), 127–151.

Gaeta, G. L., Ghinoi, S., Silvestri, F., & Tassinari, M. (2021). Innovation in the solid waste management industry: Integrating neoclassical and complexity theory perspectives. *Waste Management, 120*, 50–58.

Garcés, C., Lafuente, A., Pedraja, M., & Rivera, P. (2002). Urban waste recycling behavior: Antecedents of participation in a selective collection program. *Environmental Management, 30*(3), 378–390.

Garofalo, A., Castellano, R., Agovino, M., Punzo, G., & Musella, G. (2019). How far is campania from the best-performing region in Italy? A territorial-divide analysis of separate waste collection. *Social Indicators Research*, *142*(2), 667–688.

Guerrero, L. A., Maas, G., & Hogland, W. (2013). Solid waste management challenges for cities in developing countries. *Waste Management*, *33*(1), 220–232.

Hawkins, C. V., & Wang, X. (2012). Sustainable development governance: Citizen participation and support networks in local sustainability initiatives. *Public Works Management & Policy*, *17*(1), 7–29.

Hornsby, C., Ripa, M., Vassillo, C., & Ulgiati, S. (2017). A roadmap towards integrated assessment and participatory strategies in support of decision-making processes. The case of urban waste management. *Journal of Cleaner Production*, *142*, 157–172.

Iyamu, H. O., Anda, M., & Ho, G. (2022). Exploring the multi-level perspective in municipal solid waste management transition. *Habitat International*, *129*, 102664.

Jaeger-Erben, M., Rückert-John, J., & Schäfer, M. (2015). Sustainable consumption through social innovation: A typology of innovations for sustainable consumption practices. *Journal of Cleaner Production*, *108*, 784–798.

Joseph, K. (2006). Stakeholder participation for sustainable waste management. *Habitat International*, *30*(4), 863–871.

Læssoe, J. (2010). Education for sustainable development, participation and socio-cultural change. *Environmental Education Research*, *16*(1), 39–57.

Lakhouit, A. (2025). Revolutionizing urban solid waste management with AI and IoT: A review of smart solutions for waste collection, sorting, and recycling. *Results in Engineering*, 104018.

Marello, M., & Helwege, A. (2018). Solid waste management and social inclusion of wastepickers: Opportunities and challenges. *Latin American Perspectives*, *45*(1), 108–129.

Marshall, R. E., & Farahbakhsh, K. (2013). Systems approaches to integrated solid waste management in developing countries. *Waste Management*, *33*(4), 988–1003.

Mazzanti, M., Montini, A., & Zoboli, R. (2008). Municipal waste generation and socioeconomic drivers: Evidence from comparing Northern and Southern Italy. *The Journal of Environment & Development*, *17*(1), 51–69.

Mazzanti, M., & Zoboli, R. (2008). Waste generation, waste disposal and policy effectiveness: Evidence on decoupling from the European Union. *Resources, Conservation and Recycling*, *52*(10), 1221–1234.

McCormick, K., Anderberg, S., Coenen, L., & Neij, L. (2013). Advancing sustainable urban transformation. *Journal of Cleaner Production*, *50*, 1–11.

Mihai, F. C., Gündoğdu, S., Markley, L. A., Olivelli, A., Khan, F. R., Gwinnett, C., & Molinos-Senante, M. (2021). Plastic pollution, waste management issues, and circular economy opportunities in rural communities. *Sustainability*, *14*(1), 20.

Mmereki, D., Baldwin, A., & Li, B. (2016). A comparative analysis of solid waste management in developed, developing and lesser developed countries. *Environmental Technology Reviews*, *5*(1), 120–141.

Musella, G., Agovino, M., Casaccia, M., & Crociata, A. (2019). Evaluating waste collection management: the case of macro-areas and municipalities in Italy. *Environment, Development and Sustainability*, *21*(6), 2857–2889.

Mutatkar, R. K. (1995). Public health problems of urbanization. *Social Science & Medicine*, *41*(7), 977–981.

Nandy, S., Fortunato, E., & Martins, R. (2022). Green economy and waste management: An inevitable plan for materials science. *Progress in Natural Science: Materials International*, *32*(1), 1–9.

Nkwachukwu, O. I., Chidi, N. I., & Charles, K. O. (2010). Issues of roadside disposal habit of municipal solid waste, environmental impacts and implementation of sound management practices in developing country 'Nigeria'. *International Journal of Environmental Science and Development*, *1*(5), 409–418.

Obirih-Opareh, N., & Post, J. (2002). Quality assessment of public and private modes of solid waste collection in Accra, Ghana. *Habitat International*, *26*(1), 95–112.

Okeke, A. O., Mohammed, U., & Garba, S. (2024). Evaluation of communication interventions for improved waste management system in Nigeria. *International Journal of Sub-Saharan African Research*, 2(1), 81–95.

Owusu, G. (2010). Social effects of poor sanitation and waste management on poor urban communities: A neighborhood-specific study of Sabon Zongo, Accra. *Journal of Urbanism*, *3*(2), 145–160.

Pierini, V. I., Mazzeo, N., Cazenave, M., & Semmartin, M. (2021). Waste generation and pro-environmental behaviors at household level: A citizen science study in Buenos Aires (Argentina). *Resources, Conservation and Recycling*, *170*, 105560.

Prata, J., Simões, C. L., & Simoes, R. (2025). Improvements to municipal solid waste collection systems using real-time monitoring. *Sustainability*, *17*(4), 1405.

Pujara, Y., Pathak, P., Sharma, A., & Govani, J. (2019). Review on Indian Municipal Solid Waste Management practices for reduction of environmental impacts to achieve sustainable development goals. *Journal of Environmental Management*, *248*, 109238.

Puvača, N., Simin, M. T., Bursić, V., Đurić, K., Brkić, I., & Soleša, K. (2025). Economy, European policies, and citizens' behavior: Managing solid waste as a resource. *Journal of Agronomy, Technology and Engineering Management*, *8*(1), 1309–1321.

Romano, G., Lombardi, G. V., Rapposelli, A., & Gastaldi, M. (2022). The factors affecting Italian provinces' separate waste-collection rates: An empirical investigation. *Waste Management*, *139*, 217–226.

Salvati, L., & Carlucci, M. (2011). The economic and environmental performances of rural districts in Italy: Are competitiveness and sustainability compatible targets? *Ecological Economics*, *70*(12), 2446–2453.

Salvati, L., & Carlucci, M. (2014). A composite index of sustainable development at the local scale: Italy as a case study. *Ecological Indicators*, *43*, 162–171.

Salvati, L., Morelli, V. G., Rontos, K., & Sabbi, A. (2013). Latent exurban development: City expansion along the rural-to-urban gradient in growing and declining regions of southern Europe. *Urban Geography*, *34*(3), 376–394.

Seifollahi-Aghmiuni, S., Kalantari, Z., Egidi, G., Gaburova, L., & Salvati, L. (2022). Urbanisation-driven land degradation and socioeconomic challenges in peri-urban areas: Insights from Southern Europe. *Ambio*, *51*(6), 1446–1458.

Sharma, H. B., Vanapalli, K. R., Cheela, V. S., Ranjan, V. P., Jaglan, A. K., Dubey, B., & Bhattacharya, J. (2020). Challenges, opportunities, and innovations for effective solid waste management during and post COVID-19 pandemic. *Resources, Conservation and Recycling*, *162*, 105052.

Sharma, H. B., Vanapalli, K. R., Samal, B., Cheela, V. S., Dubey, B. K., & Bhattacharya, J. (2021). Circular economy approach in solid waste management system to achieve UN-SDGs: Solutions for post-COVID recovery. *Science of the Total Environment*, *800*, 149605.

Shevchenko, T., Laitala, K., & Danko, Y. (2019). Understanding consumer E-waste recycling behavior: Introducing a new economic incentive to increase the collection rates. *Sustainability*, *11*(9), 2656.

Singh, D., Dikshit, A. K., & Kumar, S. (2024). Smart technological options in collection and transportation of municipal solid waste in urban areas: A mini review. *Waste Management & Research*, *42*(1), 3–15.

Srivastav, A. L., & Kumar, A. (2021). An endeavor to achieve sustainable development goals through floral waste management: A short review. *Journal of Cleaner Production*, *283*, 124669.

Subri, U. S., Ghani, N. M., Rus, R. C., & Affandi, H. M. (2025). Waste no more: Empowering communities through education and participation in sustainable waste management. *Multidisciplinary Reviews*, *8*(7), 2025204–2025204.

Tansel, B. (2017). From electronic consumer products to e-wastes: Global outlook, waste quantities, recycling challenges. *Environment International*, *98*, 35–45.

Vardopoulos, I., Tsilika, E., Sarantakou, E., Zorpas, A. A., Salvati, L., & Tsartas, P. (2021). An integrated SWOT-PESTLE-AHP model assessing sustainability in adaptive reuse projects. *Applied Sciences*, *11*(15), 7134.

Velis, C. A., Wilson, D. C., Rocca, O., Smith, S. R., Mavropoulos, A., & Cheeseman, C. R. (2012). An analytical framework and tool ('InteRa') for integrating the informal recycling sector in waste and resource management systems in developing countries. *Waste Management & Research*, *30*(9S), 43–66.

Printed and bound by CPI Group (UK) Ltd, Croydon, CR0 4YY

20/08/2026

14946502-0004